THE CAIRN TERRIER

TS-216

Facing page: *Cairn puppies owned by John and Nancy Cassel.*

Overleaf: **Wee Geordie Bit O'Divil** *at 17 months. Owner and photographer, Janis Whitcomb.*

Distributed in the UNITED STATES to the Pet Trade by T.F.H. Publications, Inc., One T.F.H. Plaza, Neptune City, NJ 07753; distributed in the UNITED STATES to the Bookstore and Library Trade by National Book Network, Inc. 4720 Boston Way, Lanham MD 20706; in CANADA to the Pet Trade by H & L Pet Supplies Inc., 27 Kingston Crescent, Kitchener, Ontario N2B 2T6; Rolf C. Hagen Ltd., 3225 Sartelon Street, Montreal 382 Quebec; in CANADA to the Book Trade by Vanwell Publishing Ltd., 1 Northrup Crescent, St. Catharines, Ontario L2M 6P5 ; in ENGLAND by T.F.H. Publications, PO Box 15, Waterlooville PO7 6BQ; in AUSTRALIA AND THE SOUTH PACIFIC by T.F.H. (Australia), Pty. Ltd., Box 149, Brookvale 2100 N.S.W., Australia; in NEW ZEALAND by Brooklands Aquarium Ltd. 5 McGiven Drive, New Plymouth, RD1 New Zealand; in Japan by T.F.H. Publications, Japan—Jiro Tsuda, 10-12-3 Ohjidai, Sakura, Chiba 285, Japan; in SOUTH AFRICA by Lopis (Pty) Ltd., P.O. Box 39127, Booysens, 2016, Johannesburg, South Africa. Published by T.F.H. Publications, Inc.
MANUFACTURED IN THE UNITED STATES OF AMERICA
BY T.F.H. PUBLICATIONS, INC.

THE
CAIRN TERRIER

by Chris Carter

Cairn Terrier owned by Diane M. Blair.

Contents

Dedication

To all of those who have worked to breed responsibly and to preserve the heritage, health and soundness of the Cairn Terrier.

Acknowledgments

So many people contributed to this book that it would be impossible to name them all. However, special thanks must go to Bob Williams for the generous loan of his entire library of rare books on Cairn Terriers, to Dan Kiedrowski of *Terrier Type Magazine,* and to all the breeder/exhibitors who sent pictures and shared their time, experience and knowledge.

This little cowpoke is owned by JoAnn McLaughlin of Texas. Photograph by Missy Yuhl.

About the Author

Chris Carter obtained her first Cairn Terrier, Roylaines Bramble Bee, in 1981 and has been involved with the breed ever since. She began exhibiting Cairns in 1982 and started a small but serious breeding program soon thereafter. Cairns from her kennel are now Group and Specialty Best of Breed winners, Sweepstakes winners, and winners dog and bitch at various specialties across the country.

In addition to breeding and exhibiting Cairns, Chris has written a humorous column for *The Cairn Terrier Magazine* for over ten years and also has contributed to the Cairn breed column in the AKC *Gazette.* Recently she was approved by the AKC to judge Cairns as well. She is a member of The Cairn Terrier Club of America as well as several regional clubs.

The author and one of her Cairns hiking in the mountains.

In order to support her hobby, Chris works for a highly specialized national search firm as founding vice-president and executive search consultant. Chris lives in the mountains of central Colorado with her husband Ken, a psychologist and community college faculty member. In their spare time they enjoy sailing and spending time in their mountain home, which they share with several Cairns, an Australian Cattle Dog, and a Border Terrier.

Above left: *The author's husband Ken taking a boat ride with Moonie.* Above right: *The author with her pack.* Below: *Owner-handled by the author,* **Bramblewood's Kitty Hawk** *took Winners Bitch and Best of Winners at her first show—a specialty!*

The History of the Breed

EARLY HISTORY

No one knows for sure exactly where the Cairn Terrier originated or when this momentous event occurred. Even the earliest fanciers who brought this little dog with the big personality to the forefront of the terrier world did not agree on his origins. Some claim he first appeared in the misty isles of the North of Scotland; the Isle of Skye is often mentioned. Others rooted for the western coastal areas with their rocky shores. Probably both of these are correct to some degree.

According to popular belief, the Cairn Terrier is the oldest of the short-legged terriers and the foundation for other breeds such as the Scottish Terrier and the West Highland White Terrier. Of course, Scottie and Westie people might disagree.

What is known is that for centuries a hardy, short-legged dog was bred by gamekeepers and crofters in the northern reaches of Scotland. This little dog was of no distinct breed. Some had prick ears, some ears were dropped. Most had harsh, weather-resistant coats. They were small, hard–working dogs who earned their living by hunting everything from rats to badgers. They were not bred for looks but for gameness in going to ground. A dog who would not go into a tunnel in the earth or a rocky cairn after vermin twice his size was not considered worthy. It is said that many of these little

Chs. Redletter Elford Mhorag, Redletter McRuffie and *Ch. Redletter McMurran.* McMurran was the first Cairn to go BIS at an English championship event.

"earth dogs" were without the tips of their noses, a disfigurement caused by underground encounters from which they emerged victorious but scarred. This was considered a badge of honor. However, it also led to a common misconception that Cairns were bred to go to ground and kill their prey when in fact it was more desirable for them to bolt the vermin for the huntsmen to destroy. Their loud barking, still very much in evidence today, let their masters know where they were underground as they worked their quarry.

Some of the first written evidence of small working terriers, which could have been the forerunners of the modern Cairn, are mentioned in several books by early fanciers, a list of which is included in the bibliography of this book. Letters dating back to the 1600s also mention these little dogs.

Records kept by old Scottish families such as the Macdonalds of Waternish, the McLeods of Drynoch, and the kennel of McKinnon of Kilbride back in the 1800s would seem to indicate the breeding of dogs who were quite possibly the foundation of the breed as we know it today. In these times, every lord of the manor, or laird as he was known, had his pack of terriers or *cuallach de madaidhean*. The

Ch. Guynach Cachunn with Colonel Whitehead and his wife in the early 1920s.

gamekeepers of the estates had their *Madah* or house dogs. Even the house dogs had to show their worth and earn their supper.

In the early 1900s, fanciers other than lairds and crofters began seriously breeding the highland terriers. Among the first to work for official recognition was Mrs. Alastair Campbell. She became enamored with the little dogs on her visits to the highlands and obtained breeding stock. The first entries of dogs presumed to be Cairns appeared in the June, 1907 issue of the *Kennel Gazette*.

These dogs, owned by Mrs. Campbell, were Calla Mhor and Cuillean Bhan, both out of the same bitch but with different sires. Later that year, the registry included Mrs. Campbell's Roy Mhor, who later became one of the first Cairns exhibited at a show and who sired one of the first Challenge Certificate winners. Obviously, Mrs. Campbell intended to begin exhibition of the "new" breed by registering these dogs. The dogs were at that time registered under the heading of Prick-eared Skye Terriers.

At the Inverness and North of Scotland Canine Society shows on the 23 and 24 of September, 1909, the Cairn was first exhibited under Judge Theo Marples, the editor of *Our Dogs.* Mrs. Campbell entered three dogs, Roy Mohr, Doran Bhan, and McLeod of McLeod. There was also a bitch present, Fassie, who took first prize. This bitch was handled by Mrs. Campbell and owned by Mrs. Macdonald.

In 1910 the Kennel Club moved registration from "Prick-eared Skye Terrier" to "Any other breed or variety" and 35 dogs were registered. The popularity of the breed was already growing by leaps and bounds. In October, 1911 an official standard was drawn up at the Scottish Kennel Club Show in Edinburgh. It is interesting to follow the development of the standard itself through the years that followed. By 1912 the Kennel Club began awarding Challenge Certificates and gave the Cairn Terrier a separate register.

Mrs. Campbell was by no means alone in her love of the Cairn Terrier. Other early fanciers worked hard to further the breed. Among their numbers were many whose names are easily recognizable to any serious fancier today: Mr. Macdonald of Waternish, Mr. McLeod, the Honorable Mary Hawke, the Lady Sophie Scott, Lady Charles Bentinck, Mrs. Florence M. Ross, Mrs. Fleming, Mr. A. Wallace, the Baroness Burton, Lt. Colonel Whitehead, and Mrs. Dixon.

As time passed, more and more Cairns were entered in shows. The first two Cairns to win Challenge Certificates were Firring Fling and Firring Flora, both owned by Mrs. Ross and Mrs. Markland. It was only fitting that Mrs. Alastair Campbell judged this show, which was held in Richmond in 1912. The next two to win Challenge Certificates were Skye Crofter and Lady Sophie Scott's Tibbie of Harris. Later that year, a new dog bred by Mr. M. McKinnon and owned by Mrs. Campbell was put up. His name was Gesto. His sire was Sgithanach Bhan, a dog who was either a white Cairn or a West Highland White Terrier, depending on who was discussing him. Breeding so-called white Cairns and the interbreeding of Cairns and Westies was acceptable in those days. An end was put to this practice as of January 1, 1925.

Ch. Redletter McBryan was the top producer of the breed until 1984.

The first Cairn Terrier champion was confirmed in 1913 at Birmingham. The judge, Mr. W. Goodall Copestake, awarded the third Challenge Certificate to the bitch Tibbie of Harris, owned by Lady Sophie Scott. How thrilled Lady Scott must have felt to have received such an honor. To be sure, Tibbie's main thrill was in pleasing her mistress.

The first dog champion was Gesto, bred by Mr. Mckinnon. Later in the year, championships were attained by Skye Crofter, Firring Frolic, and another Lady Scott bitch, Shiela of Harris.

The year 1914 brought more registrations, more entries at shows, more Challenge Certificates, more champions, and more interest in the breed. Ch. Firring Frolic won five Challenge Certificates, more than any other Cairn that year. This outstanding dog was a red brindle whose sire and dam were unregistered. All told, this dog won 11 Challenge Certificates before World War I brought dog shows to a virtual halt.

According to Edward C. Ash in his book *The Cairn Terrier*, first published in 1936, eight dogs and six bitches finished their championships by the end of 1914. The dogs were Gesto, Skye Crofter, Firring Frolic, Firring Fox, Mearach, Northern Nonpareil, Rockfield Simon, and Sporran. The bitches were Tibbie of Harris, Brocaire Sperieag, Langley Tiggy,

Ch. Redletter McJoe, owned and bred by W.N. Bradshaw, made a great name for himself as a winner and an even greater one as a producer.

numbers of registrations and Cairns exhibited. Americans and Canadians were becoming interested in the breed as well.

Prominent in the show ring were the original fanciers as well as the newcomers. Baroness Burton's Dochfour kennels did well and Mrs. Campbell was ever present with her Brocaire dogs. Mr. MacLennan's Cairngowan dogs won well, as did Mrs. Fleming's Out of the West Cairns. By 1923, over 1000 Cairns were registered. The Harviestoun kennels began to make their mark, especially the stud dog Harviestoun Raider who was the product of known but unregistered parents. Miss Dixon's Gunthorpe dogs were providing strong competition. By the end of 1924, probably the most winning Cairns were Mrs. Fleming's dog Fisherman Out of the West and the bitch Fury Out of the West. The Out of the West Cairns continued to dominate the show ring into 1927. Fisherman had eight Challenge Certificates with the nearest competition being Mrs. Campbell's Brocaire Jura winning four.

Maisie of Harris, Rona, and Shiela of Harris. Mr. Ash noted not only the importance of these dogs in the history of the breed but the importance of the early judges, most of whom were breeders. A look at early judging records shows a great deal of variation in placement of the same dogs at different shows. These breeder/judges had tremendous influence on the future of the breed. Their opinions determined which dogs were used more at stud and which bitches were bred to whom. To a certain degree, this influence of judges still holds true today.

When World War I began, dog shows were a luxury that fell by the wayside. Registration of Cairns fell dramatically as more pressing concerns took precedence. However, immediately after the end of the War, fanciers made up for lost time with record

An interesting story from Mrs.

Fleming's kennels is that of Fury Out of the West. According to Mr. Edward Ash in his book *The Cairn Terrier*, Fury was never bred, as Mrs. Fleming considered her too old when she finished her show career. She only weighed ten pounds when she won her first Challenge Certificate. Today it is hard to imagine a bitch of this size even being considered in the ring. Fury died in 1932 after being diagnosed with a tumor.

In Mrs. Fleming's own words, "rather than risk complications and suffering, I sent her painlessly from me, and she went as we all remember her, brave to the last, head and tail up, and one who never let me down." Fisherman Out of the West had died earlier in an accident. Both dogs were missed in the ring where they always caused a sensation.

While the Out of the West Kennel continued to win steadily clear into the 1930s, newcomers began to make their mark. The kennel names of Carysford, Mercia, and Hyver were often attached to winning Cairns.

Probably the most influential

sire of the early days was Harviestoun Raider, whelped in November of 1919. He was not a dog to win consistently at shows and was not shown often. He had too much substance for the ring, but it stood him in good stead as a sire. He passed along all of his good qualities, stamping his offspring with his best attributes. His son, Harviestoun Brigand, carried on his legacy as a sire. In all, Raider produced 11 champions. While today, especially in the United States, that number does not seem large, for his time it was unprecedented. An examination of pedigrees of Challenge Certificate-winning Cairns will show that Raider was in the background of at least two-thirds of them.

Ch. Splinters of Twobees. A foundation sire in many modern lines, he is the "S" in line DGS.

15

Left: *Mrs. Alastair Campbell and her winning Cairn Terrier Gesto. Photo, 1912, J. Russell & Sons, Old Bond Street.* Above: *The Baroness Burton with* **Dochfour Vennach, Ch. Ross-shire Warrior,** *and* **Ch. Dochfour Kyle.** *Photo, Sport & General,* Our Dogs, *Dec. 8, 1922.*

It is interesting to note that Raider had strong West Highland White Terrier in his own pedigree, especially through his sire's side.

His grandsire and both great-grandsires were Westies, although some claimed them to be white Cairns. On his dam's side was Sgithanach Bhan, the West Highland White (or white Cairn) who had sired Ch. Gesto.

The home of the "DOCHFOUR" Cairn Terriers. Photo, Sport & General, Our Dogs, *Dec. 8, 1922.*

The "Canton Bay" Cairn Terriers, Our Dogs, Dec. 14, 1928. Miss and Master Trimmer-Thompson with the pack on the sands.

The winning "Warberry" Cairns, Our Dogs, Dec. 14, 1928. Mrs. Hoyle with **Warlock, Waterbaby**, and **Kiltie.**

The "Gunthorpe" Kennel of Cairn Terriers. Our Dogs, Dec. 4, 1931. Some of Mrs. Dixon's "Gunthorpe" Cairn Terriers out for exercise. Photo, Stephens Picture Agency.

Mr. Donald MacLennan with **Carngowan Chief, Cadora** and **Clinker.** Photo, Carl Cloud, Manchester. Our Dogs, Dec. 11, 1925.

1931 Puppies by Moccasin Magnet.

Princelo Jester. Our Dogs, 1934

The Harviestoun line owed much to Mr. Ross and his Glenmhor Cairns. These dogs were well known for their consistency of type. There was much Westie influence in these dogs and they did not win as much as others, but produced well.

Raider was not the only influential sire of the time, although he was the one most remembered. There was also Doughall Out of the West, who sired Fury. His progeny produced almost 100 Challenge Certificates among them. Ch. Breakwater Jock, a descendant of Firring Frolic, was in the pedigrees of winners. Gillie of Hyver was considered an important sire a bit later, along with Brocaire Hamish of Gesto and Raider's son, Brigand. A sire often neglected but of great importance was Ch. Trashurst Chip, the sire of Ch. Splinters of Twobees. Chip was described as a dog with a magnificent head, strong legs and feet, wonderful balance, and sound movement.

In January of 1933 the famous Ch. Splinters of Twobees made his appearance. He was descended from Hyver stock on his sire's side. While he was fairly successful in the show ring with eight Challenge Certificates, his influence on the breed as a sire was felt for years to come. Many of the leading dogs of the late 1930s and 1940s had Splinters in their pedigrees. In fact, well over 100 champions in England alone can trace their pedigrees back to Splinters in the male line.

Probably the most famous offspring of Splinters was born in 1943 with the name Sport of Zellah. This dog was bred by Mrs. E. L. Hazell but was purchased by Miss Bengough and Mrs. Butterworth who, with Kennel Club approval, changed his name to Bonfire of Twobees. This dog was bred to a bitch owned by Walter Bradshaw and the kennel name Redletter went down in history.

This particular breeding in 1948 between Bonfire of Twobees and Redletter My Choice produced Ch. Redletter McJoe, the founding sire of the famous Redletter Cairns. McJoe exerted his genetic influence on many lines of that day. His descendants are numerous in the kennels of Uniquecottage, Rossarden, Felshott, Oudenarde, and particularly Yeendsdale. McJoe produced Ch. Redletter McMurran, winner of 27 Challenge Certificates and a Best In Show.

McMurran sired Ch. Redletter McBryan, the top producer of the breed until 1984 when he was unseated by Ch. Robinson Crusoe of Courtrai. McBryan's influence was felt in many kennels including Cairncrag and Blencathra. In America, McJoe's son EngAmCan. Ch. Redletter McRuffie became one of the most important sires and genetically influential dogs in the history of the breed.

Post World War II in Great Britain

World War II put the brakes on dog showing and breeding, but once again things picked up as soon as the War ended. Immediately certain dogs made their presence felt. Bonfire of Twobees, the Splinters son, won five Challenge Certificates. The Hillston kennel name came into play with five Challenge Certificates by Hillston Ian Dhu. McJoe of Twobees also won five Challenge Certificates. Blencathra made a splash with Sandpiper and Sandboy, and Redletter became a name known throughout the Cairn world. These kennel names are all still recognized, even by novices, today.

In the late 1940s, only 24 champions were finished compared with 96 in the 1950s. The slow start after the War ended did not last long. In addition to Bonfire and McJoe of Twobees fame, Mrs. Drummond finished three of her Blencathra dogs. Ch. Blencathra Sandboy not only finished his own championship,

Ch. Oudenarde Raiding Light owned by Mrs. F.A. Somerfield of England.

Ch. Blencathra Stonechat born August 8, 1953.

Great Britain. Baroness Burton was still very much in evidence with four champions from her Dochfour kennels. Blencathra finished nine Cairns and had a strong influence on many other kennels. Mrs. Mawson's Glenmacdhui Cairns finished two champions out of Ch. Blencathra Redstart. Redstart proved to be a top producing sire with eight champions from 1950 to 1960 along with Ch. Blencathra Sandpiper who sired five.

Hillston continued well with four champions. Mrs. Yeends kennel of Yeendsdale finished six. The Lofthouse Cairns of Mrs. Manley got a good start with two champions and many more to follow. The Merrymeet Cairns of Mrs. E. F. Leverson made up six champions, tapping into Twobees and Blencathra blood lines along the way. Miss Hamilton's and Miss Temple's Oudenarde kennel finished four dogs and Mrs. Leigh's Thistleclose finished five. Miss Dixon made her start with her Ch. Rogie of Rossarden and that kennel name became a more prominent one in later years. And the Uniquecottage Cairns of Misses Judy Marshall (now Mrs. Parker-Tucker) and Hazel Longmore (now Mrs. Small of Avenelhouse fame) had a solid start in the latter part of the decade finishing three dogs and a bitch, using Redletter and

but sired one of the others who did. To this day, Blencathra dogs are known for the beautiful heads they carried and passed on.

Mrs. M. Garbutt had three champions from her Hillston kennel in the 1940s and one of her dogs sired yet another champion, Michelcombe Fay. Mmes. Hamilton and Temple finished Oudenarde Duskie Bell, a bitch bred by Mr. Coombes, starting a post-war dynasty of Oudenarde Cairns that is still influential today. The Pledwick kennel of Mrs. Summers finished one Cairn with more to come. Dogs born in that decade who did not finish then but became well-known later on included those of Toptwig, Merrymeet, and Yeendsdale.

The 1950s saw over 90 Cairn Terrier champions made up in

Thistleclose as sires.

The big story of the 1950s was that of Walter Bradshaw and his Redletter Cairns. A staggering 18 Redletter Cairns became champions from 1950 to 1959, including Ch. Redletter Miss Splinters and Ch. Redletter McJoe who sired Ch. Redletter McMurran, who in turn sired Ch. Redletter McBryan, a top sire of the breed for many years. Another McJoe son finished in 1953, Ch. Redletter McRuffie, who was exported to Canada and became a top show dog as well as a top producing sire there and in the United States. Ch. Redletter McJoe sired nine champions in great Britain between 1950 to 1959 alone. He was followed by McMurran with five. Among them, Champions McJoe of Twobees,

Bonfire of Twobees, and Splinters of Twobees sired eight champions during the same period showing Twobees as a powerful influence.

The 1960s brought continued success to the Cairn breed and to the emerging kennels of the 1950s. The sires of Redletter, Blencathra, Lofthouse, and Oudenarde made an indelible mark on the breed. Ch. Redletter McBryan sired 13 champions during the decade, while Redletter dogs including McMurran, Master Mac, Marshall, and Maestro brought the total to 27 champions sired from 1960 to 1969. Their influence, particularly through the sons of McJoe, was felt by Uniquecottege, Rossarden, Felshott, Yeendsdale, Oudenarde, Cairncrag, Blencathra, Craglyn and many others throughout the

Ch. Redletter Miss Splinters was imported from England by Betty Hyslop. Defeated only once in 60 times shown.

post-war decades.The Blencathra sires, particularly Milord and Elford Badger, produced 20 champions and contributed to the kennels of Merrymeet, Oudenarde, Pledwick, Seiyun and Craiglyn.

Lofthouse Geryon of Mistyfell, a Ch. Blencathra Redstart son, produced eight of the 12 champions sired by Lofthouse dogs in the 1960s.

Mmes. Hamilton and Temple had a successful decade with their sires producing eight

Ch. Blencathra Galgate Lady Piper born July 23, 1948.

champions. Among them were Oudenarde Midnight Chimes, and Midnight Marauder. Marauder produced EngAmCan. Ch. Oudenarde Sea Hawk, who was a significant sire in North America. Marauder also sired Oudenarde's top producer, Ch. Oudenarde Raiding Light, who was born in 1969 and won his British title in 1970. Raiding Light sired eight British champions. According to Mrs. Ferelith Hamilton Somerfield, both dogs were top class, but if she had to choose one it would have been Marauder, who sired dogs who were important to the breed on both sides of the Atlantic. He was out of what she describes as arguably one of Oudenarde's best bitches, Ch. Oudenarde Fair Prospect. Do not forget that Marauder was in competition as a stud with both his own sire, Midnight Chimes, and his grandsire, Ch. Oudenarde Sandboy, not to mention Raiding Light who was well-known in the show ring and often used at stud by those who admired him.

The Glenmacdhui Cairns of Mrs. Mawson came on strong in the sixties. Ch. Glenmacdhui Tearlach was purchased by Miss J. Hudson and became an important sire in the Clanranald line. Other new names on the scene included Miss Campbell's Craiglyn kennel and the highly successful Felshott kennel of Misses Hall and Wilson. Toptwig was another new name on the dog show scene. Mrs. G. Marsh finished four Toptwig champions.

Ch. Blencathra Barrie born May 7, 1967.

Ch. Blencathra Sandpiper born October 26, 1944.

tremendous impact on the Cairns in the United States.

In the years since the sixties, the kennels established then have made their mark on the breed in both Great Britain and North America. Early on in the seventies, Avenelhouse made its entrance. While this was a new kennel prefix, its holder was no stranger to the Cairn world. Mrs. Hazel Small, nee Longmore, had been a partner in the Uniquecottage kennel for many years, but upon her marriage to Major Small she decided to branch off on her own. Miss Marshall, now Mrs. Judith Parker-Tucker, kept the Uniquecottage prefix and continues to successfully breed and exhibit Cairns to this day. Both of these ladies had a tremendous influence on the breed both with their dogs and with their willingness to share information and assistance with newcomers.

While the Blencathra dogs did not make as strong a showing in the ring that they had in the past, their studs, particularly Elford Badger and Brat, had a strong impact, siring ten champions.

Mrs. Harding's Brucairns were quite successful in the ring, finishing eight champions, matched by Misses Hall & Wilson's Felshott Cairns. Felshott Honey Badger was a stud whose impact was felt well into the early 1980s. Ch. Heshe Donovan finished his championship, among other Heshe Cairns. In addition to

Still going well were Mrs. Leverton's Merrymeet kennels, the Vinovium dogs of Mrs. Jagger, and Miss Dixon's Rossarden Cairns. The first Heshe Cairn finished her championship during this time. This name is important in that a bit later on, Mr. F.A. Edwards bred a litter out of Drusilla of Rossarden sired by Ch. Blencathra Brat which produced Ch. Heshe Donovan. Donovan became the sire of the top producing Cairn in Great Britain to date, Ch. Robinson Crusoe of Courtrai, who has also had a siring the top producer of all time in Great Britain, Ch. Robinson Crusoe of Courtrai, he sired Ch. Early Bird of Uniquecottage, a top producing bitch. Courtrai Cairns got off to a good start and still are going strong in the 90s.

Mr. Bradshaw's Redletter Cairns continued to dominate both in shows and in the whelping box. Redletter finished a dozen champions and well over 15 champions were sired by the kennel studs, mostly by Moonstruck, Michael, and Magic Orb. Other active and well-known kennels included Toptwig, Clanranald, Thimswara, Pledwick, Twinlaw, Vinovium, Seltkirk, CamCairn and Rossarden, and Ljekarna.

In the late 70s and early 80s, several new prefixes began showing up in the winner's ring. Clanranald Cairns did well. Miss Jean Hudson had one champion, Ch. Clanranald Tam O'Shanter, who was exported to the United States where he finished his AKC championship and sired champions. The Glenbrae prefix of Mr. Ian Kettle made its appearance, as did Mrs. Robinson's Cruzo. Others quite familiar to today's exhibitors include Mrs. Spence's Harlight Cairns, the Larchlea prefix of Mrs. Templeton, Mr. David Wright's Ljekarna dogs going back into Foxgrove lines, Mrs. Shuttleworth's Monary dogs, the Penticharm Cairns of Mr. and Mrs. Hooton, and Mrs. Sally Ogle's Pinetop Cairns.

Ch. Hamish of Seltirk, the last GB champion to gain his title. Owned by Mrs. Proudlock of Scotland.

"Newcomers," meaning those who began breeding and exhibiting in the past ten or 20 years, also include Mr. J. Alexander with his Ugadale Cairns, Mr. Bunting with Spirecairn, and Mr. Pollock with the Standyke prefix. Mrs. Breach's Hearn Cairns have appeared in pedigrees on both continents.

Ch. Sehottische of Seltirk won Best of Breed at Crufts in 1977. Owned by Mrs. Proudlock of Scotland.

Many Cairns in the U.S. and Canada can trace their pedigrees to these newer "kids" on the block. But never forget that they have their roots in the more established lines and all these dogs can trace their origins back to the pioneers of the breed.

The latter 1980s found all of these exhibitors doing well and even a few more newcomers. Brindleoaks made its appearance and Mr. Holme's Ch. Brindleoaks Buck was a top Challenge Certificate winner along with Mrs.

Ch. Foxgrove Jeronimo with owner H.G. Wilkinson.

Weinberger and Miss Frances' Ch. Correnie Stormkeeper. Mr. and Mrs. Croyman finished three champions and Miss Catto's Birselaw's Cairns made their debut with two champions. Ch. Larchlea Here's Harvey was a top Challenge Certificate winner in the late 80s. Mr. and Mrs. Firth finished two Cairngold Cairns, including a popular sire Ch. Cairngold Kramer. Kinkim finished three Cairns; HoneyHall made up two. The early 90s have given us some exciting Cairns. Ch. Corbieha Hazelnut, a bitch with well over 25 Challenge Certificates, is the bitch Challenge Certificates record-holder. Ch. Larchlea Take a Chance on Me has been an all-time top winner along with Mrs. Sander's Ch. Beaudesert Royal Viking. Who knows where these newer Cairns will end up in the history books. They are part of history currently being made.

Not to be forgotten are the top producing dams. Obviously stud dogs are able to produce more champions than bitches. The average bitch, if bred three times, will produce somewhere between six to 12 puppies. As difficult as it is to complete a championship in Great Britain, any bitch who has produced multiple champions should be highly celebrated.

Dams who have produced four champions (as of 1989) include Ch. Felshott Bryany, Foundation Sylvia, Ch. Felshott Anita, Ch. Early Bird of Uniquecottage, Ch. Redletter Marcel, and Ch.

Ch. Cairngold Crackerjack *was the sire of several American champions. Owned by Redcoat Cairns, Jack & Karen Smith*

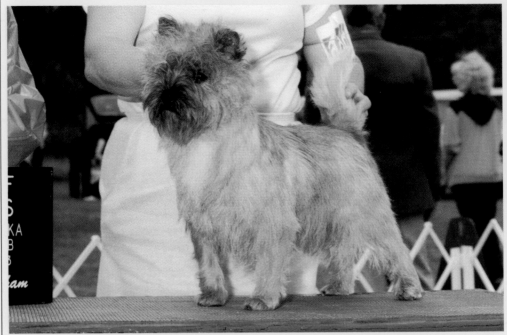

Cairngold Carmen of Uniquecottage, an English import to the U.S. Owner, Betty Marcum.

Ch. Harlight Honeysuckle owned by Mrs. L.Z. Spence.

Lofthouse Geryon, *imported to the U.S. by Don Robbie.*

Ch. Larchlea Take A Chance On Me J.W. *Best of Breed at Crufts in 1990 and 1991 and Best in Show winner at the Scottish Breeds General Championship Show in 1991. Owned by Mrs. C. Templeton.*

Courtrai Triella Trudy. Special mention goes to Ch. Felshott Araminta who produced three champions, all in one litter, sired by Ch. Redletter Maestro. It is also interesting to note that all of these top producing dams were from line DGS which is now the dominating line in Cairn Terriers on both sides of the Atlantic.

LINES AND FAMILIES

It was common practice among race-horse owners in the early 1900s to keep track of their pedigrees using a system which coded dominant sires and dams. While not scientifically accurate, the system allowed an owner or breeder to track his stock back to

their origins and make projections of breeding trends. Dr. Rosslyn Bruce, a terrier fancier, persuaded some of the terrier breeders to adopt the system. The Rev. and Mrs. Casperz, Cairn enthusiasts, took to it wholeheartedly and began tracking the Cairn Terrier breed. Later Mr. Alex Fisher recorded every Cairn Challenge Certificate winner back six generations and every entry in the Kennel Club Stud Books to three generations in alphabetical order. Mrs. Bunty Proudlock kept the records up to date and they are still available and actively used in Great Britain and, to a lesser degree, in the United States.

Male lines in a pedigree are

annotated by letters indicating the original foundation sires in tail male (the top line of the pedigree) descent.

While lines are denoted by the tail male, families are the province of bitches and are annotated by numbers, traced through the dams on the bottom line of the pedigree. This is called the tail female line.

In the early days there were four main male lines in evidence, given the letters D, G, SD, and I. The D line came to us from the original sire Duan. Among the descendants of this line were Ch. Gillie of Hyver and through him

the D influence was felt in such kennels as Twobees and Redletter.

The D line was further divided into sub-categories to indicate direct descendants through particular sires. DR originated with Duan through Raeburn Conas. DF came directly from Firring Fling. DG indicated the direct descendants of Gillie of Hyver down from Raeburn Conas. Only later was DGS added when Splinters of Twobees proved to be such a strong influence on the breed. The initials are for Duan, the originator, through Gillie and Splinters. It is this line that predominates the entire Cairn

Ch. Coalacre Milliner is an English import sired by a top producer, Ch. Cairngold Kramer. Owner, Louise Hooper.

world today.

The G line had its roots in Glenmhor and Harviestoun, with the founder being Glenmhor Pride. This line was also subdivided into GB for Ch. Harviestoun Brigand, GC for Ch. Harviestoun Chieftain, GF for Harviestoun Forgie, and GR for the descendants of Harviestoun Raider. It should be noted that Chieftain and Forgie were Raider's sons.

The SD line owes its greatest debt to Doughall Out of the West, although the foundation sire was Shona. Therefore the initials SD stand for the first letters of their names.

Oudenarde Man Of Steel by Ch. Oudenarde What Next. Photo by Jon Montgomery.

Ch. Oudenarde Fancy Light owned by Miss F.A. Hamilton. Photograph by Sally Anne Thompson.

Doughall's progeny did a great deal of winning in the early years and their genes impacted several kennels, including Shinnel. This line, along with most of the others, has lost much of its influence through the years.

Line I, its founder Iver, was greatly influenced by Ross-Shire Glenara (branch IG) and his son Ch. Ross-Shire Warrior. This line was less concentrated than the others and is somewhat more difficult to trace in modern Cairns, as so many kennels carry it under different kennel names.

While these four lines have proven their strength over time, the other lines which have faded out should be listed as they were delineated by Rev. and Mrs. Caspersz originally:

A Scottish Cairn with her two sons flanking her. Courtesy of Sybil Berrecloth.

Line A –Founded on Ames.

Line B –Founded on Badger with Branch BD going through Gesto.

Line C –Founded on Cluaran.

Line J –Founded on Jack through Ferracher and Skye Crofter.

Line SK –Founded on Skye with Firring Fox and Sgiteach Dearg Out of the West.

Line SN –Founded on Snipe of Harris.

Line T –Founded on Tony.

On the bitch side, it becomes even more difficult to track. Families producing one or more champions number well over 100. It is interesting that of the first 89 families to be numbered, six were founded on Westie bitches.

Records and names of many of the earliest bitches are lost to time, so we cannot be sure if some of these families might actually be linked through one bitch. Since bitches produce a limited number of puppies in their breeding lives, their influence is not as widely felt nor as dominant as a well-used stud dog.

Ch. Craiglyn Christmas Carol owned by Mr. and Mrs. Taylor Coleman.

Breed History in the United States

Even as recent as events in the early 1900s may seem, there is no conclusive evidence as to the first Cairns brought over from Great Britain. Credit has been given to Mrs. Henry Price of Connecticut for importing the first "known" Cairns in 1913. John T. Marvin in his book *The New Complete Cairn Terrier* states that Mrs. Price imported Sandy Peter Out of the West and Loch Scolter's Podge. Sandy Peter was the first AKC-registered Cairn. Mrs. Price remained active in Cairns for several years. By 1914, the first American-bred Cairn was registered, Lorne Spirag, bred and owned by Mrs. H. W. Warden.

It was not long before a club was formed. In the fall of 1917 it had six members, growing dramatically as the popularity of the Cairn Terrier took off. By 1918 the United States had its first Champion Cairn Terrier. He was an import, Greentree Ardsheal Gille Cam, owned by Mrs. Payne Whitney. In fact, for many years most Cairns finishing their championships in United States were imports.

Another early fancier, Mrs. Byron Rogers, became active in the breed and was one of the early U.S. club members. She wrote the first book in the U.S. about Cairn and Sealyham Terriers, having an interest in both breeds. This book gives us the first copy of the standard of points used at that time.

Ch. Greentree Ardsheal Gillie Cam, owned by Mrs. Payne Whitney, was the first American champion of the breed.

There were other early fanciers, but probably the most famous and influential ones made their appearance in the 1920s. These included the Tennants, the Wards, Mrs. Loomis, and the Harlans. The most recognizable people at this time, and for years to follow, had to be Mrs. Amy Bacon of Cairnvreckan and Mr. & Mrs. Lindsley Tappin, who had the famous Tapscott kennels. A look at early title holders found these two kennels, particularly Tapscott, dominated the American-bred scene.

*Mrs. Kenneth Harlan holds her bitch, **Jinx Ballantrae,** a Best in Show winner. Photo by Lester Rounds.*

There were many others who held their share of the limelight and kept the breed in the public eye. Miss Helen Hunt and her Shagbark Cairns appeared in the 1930s and continued well after the Second World War. She imported, among others, Ch. Simon of Twobees, and by the mid 1950s she had finished over 30 champions. She assisted many newcomers to the breed over the years. The Killybracken kennel of Mrs. Groverman Ellis was active at the same time. Not only did Mrs. Ellis attain championships of over 35 Cairns but she put obedience titles on many of them as well. Melita, the Canadian kennel of Mrs. L. M. Wood, showed its first Cairns in the 1930s and continued for many years. After WWII, the Melita dogs became better known and can be found on many modern pedigrees. Mrs. R. T. Allen's Craigdu kennels were active for over 45 years. Mr. and Mrs. Carl Brewer began showing their Heathcairn dogs around 1950. Their Ch. Heathcairn Cuthbert was a foundation sire for the Bairdsain Cairns of Mr. and Mrs. Charles Norris.

While there are far too many kennels to discuss in detail or even to name in a general book such as this, there are a few which have had such an impact on the breed that they must be

Ch. Cairnwoods Quince was a silver puppy who darkened over the years. He is shown here at seven months. Photo by E.M. Shafer.

mentioned. Dogs bred, exhibited, or imported by these kennels have gone down in history as some of the "greats." And while the top winners are certainly important, even more important are the top producers these kennels owned.

In the 1930s a newcomer to Cairns, Mrs. Betty Hyslop of Ontario, Canada joined the crowd and became one of the most well-known breeders on the northern continent. She purchased her first American show dogs from Tapscott in 1930. She also imported many dogs from Great Britain. The first was Placemore Peekaboo, followed by Eng. Ch.

Seaworthy Out of the West. Mrs. Hyslop was a key to making some of the finest British lines available to breeders in Canada and the United States. The importance of this cannot be stressed enough. Without these imported sires, Cairns as we know them today would not exist.

Among the most influential dogs to be imported by Mrs. Hyslop was the Splinters' descendant, a grandson of the great Eng. Ch. Redletter McJoe, the EngAmCan. Ch. Redletter McRuffie. Mrs. Hyslop brought him to the northern continent in 1953. He promptly began an impressive winning streak including BOB at Westminster and BOB at the 1955 and 1956 Cairn Terrier Club of America specialties. In reviewing the pedigrees of North American champions, McRuffie clearly merits ranking as one of the most powerful influences on the breed in history. In his line of descendants you will find the likes of Ch. Caithness Rufus, Ch. Cairnwoods Quince, Ch. Cairmar Fancy Dresser, Ch. Cairmar Scot Free, Ch. Cairmar Connecticut Yankee, Ch. Cairnwoods Golden Boy, Ch. Caithness Fays Falcon, Ch. Whetstone Halston, Ch. Cairndania McBrigand's Brigrey, Ch. Caithness Barnabas, Ch. Tradorohg's Dunstan Claymore, CDX, Ch. Whistle Gate Glen Fiddich II, Ch. Gayla Cairn's Davey, and Ch. Gayla Cairn's Gregor McKim to name only a few of the top producers of our time. Entire kennels were based on the sons, daughters, grandsons, and granddaughters of McRuffie.

Other important sires imported by Mrs. Hyslop included EngAmCan. Ch. Oudenarde Sea Hawk, who sired her successful AmCan. Ch. Rogerlyn Sea Hawk's Salty Sam. Sam won 11 Best in Show awards, a record at that time. Another import who did well for Mrs. Hyslop was EngAmCan. Ch. Redletter Twinlaw Seaspirit. Others included EngAmCan. Ch's Redletter McBrigand and Lofthouse Davey.

Males were not the only imports. AmCan. Ch. Foxgrove Susanella was a show-stopper with her beautiful Blencathra head and sound movement. She won seven Best In Show awards in Canada, one in the U.S. and was the Cairn Terrier Club of America BOB in 1974.

A more recent but equally important imported sire was Ch. Foxgrove Jeronimo. Jeronimo was not only a critical sire in the continuing saga of Cairndania but a top show dog as well. He and

Ch. Redletter McBrigand, owned by Mrs. Betty Hyslop. Photo by Rudolph Tauskey.

Above: *Ch. Caithness Rufus,* owned by Mrs. Ralph Stone. Below: *Rufus came to the attention of the Cairn fancy quite early in his show career. As a puppy Rufus was selected Best of Breed over a large entry of top dogs at Chicago International by judge Elise Untermyer.*

his progeny continued the Cairndania winning streak at Westminster for years. You will find Jeronimo in pedigrees of Cairns all over the United States and Canada.

A competitive spirit, Mrs. Hyslop continues to be an active participant in breeding and exhibiting her Cairns to this day. She is often in the ring with one of her youngsters at specialties, bringing them along herself while delegating the exhibition of her specials to professional handlers. Her more recent winners include Ch. Foxairn Tinman, his sire Ch. Sharolaine's Kalypso, Ch. Gaelic Haggis MacBasher, Ch. Cairndania Sam's Sundew, Ch. Wee Gaelic Todd Cairndania, and Ch. Cairnmoor's T's Tammy Cairndania.

One of the most well-recognized names among prepotent sires in the history of American bred Cairn Terriers is that of Ch. Caithness Rufus. He was bred and owned by Mrs. Betty Stone. His sire was a Cairndania dog, Ch. Cairndania's

Above left:**Ch. Flair's Flirt of Wolfpit** shown going Best in Sweepstakes at the C.T.C.A. 1967 national specialty.
Above right:**Ch. Caithness Periwinkle** out of Caithness Little Bit x Caithness Sorceress. Owner, Betty Marcum.
Below:**Ch. Cairmar Colonel Peri,** a Periwinkle son and brother to Fancy That. Owned by Betty Marcum.

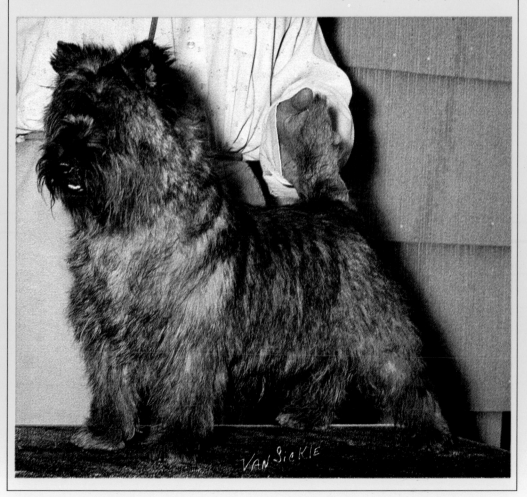

Ch. Caithness Barnabas, *sire of 33 champions. Owner, Betty Marcum.*

McRuffie's Raider, who was himself a Ch. Redletter McRuffie son. Raider was bred to Ch. Caithness Briar Rose who was out of imported stock, and the result was Rufus, a sensational show dog who became a top sire with 31 champion get to his credit. Among them were Ch. BellaCairn Black Bottom, Ch. Caithness Colonel, and Ch. Cairnwoods Golden Boy who was purchased and exhibited by Mrs. Stone when she retired Rufus. Mrs. Stone preferred to show her own dogs and did so quite successfully. She stands as an important person in the breed, not only for producing excellent Cairns but for providing the foundation stock for many of the modern kennels.

The Rufus son Ch. Caithness Golden Boy is probably most famous for his own sons, Ch. Caithness Fays Falcon and Ch. Cairnwoods Quince.

Ch. Caithness Fay's Falcon, owned by Margaret Magee of Whistle Gate Cairns, produced 16 champions of impressive quality. Falcon was the sire of Ch. Tradorogh's Dunstan Claymore, CDX, a name found in many of the Cairmar Cairns of today. Falcon's influence was strongly felt in the kennels of Brigadoon, Annwood, and Loch Katrine among others. Of course, Whistle Gate produced several champions including Ch. Whistle Gate Glen Fiddich II, a top sire in the mid-1980s on the west coast. Falcon was the grandsire of Ch. Caithness Barnabas, who was out

Ch. Caithness Fay's Falcon photographed by Missy Yuhl.

of a Rufus sister, and a top producer with 33 champions. Barnabas was another sire in the Cairmar breeding program.

Ch. Cairnwoods Quince, double Rufus grandson, is one of the two top producing Cairn sires of all time along with his great-grandson Ch. Cairmar Fancy Dresser, both with 51 Champion

Ch. Cairnwoods Golden Boy, a Rufus son and top-producing sire in his own right.

Left: *Mrs. Payne Whitney's Cairn Terrier,* **Greentree Ardsheal Gillie Cam** *was the first Cairn to become an American champion. Photo by Hopton. Below: Miss Elizabeth M. Braun (Bethcairn, Pittsburgh, PA), with some of her noted winning Cairns. Photo by Bachrach.*

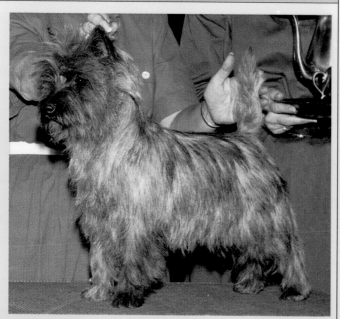

Right:***Ch. Berry Special of Wolfpit*** owned by Lydia C. Hutchinson. Below:***Ch. Milbryan Killarney O'Cairmar,*** *a most important bitch. Dam of Ch. Cairmar Connecticut Yankee and Ch. Tagalong of Wildwood. Owners, Mr. and Mrs. Robert B. Williams.*

Ch. Craiglyn Christmas Carol won Best in Show at the Cairn Terrier Club of America in 1977 when she was nearly seven years old. Owners, Mr. and Mrs. Taylor Coleman.

offspring. Quince was bred by Luanne Craco of Cairnwoods when she was only 18 years old. Quince was a half-brother to half-sister breeding of Ch. Cairnwoods Golden Boy to Caithness Gracenote. Mrs. Taylor Coleman of Wolfpit Cairns bought him as a puppy. Her daughter Lydia Coleman Hutchinson, still breeding Wolfpit Cairns today as well as being an active dog show judge, knew from the start that he was destined to be a great one. His show record was impressive: a Best in Show, well over 60 group placements, and a four-time winner of Best of Breed at the Cairn Terrier Club of America national specialty. His last win at this show was in 1980 from the Veterans class at over 12 years of age.

Wolfpit is one of the kennels that deserves special mention. It was founded in 1939 as the result of a gift to the Colemans of a black-brindle bitch puppy, Kiltie of Wolfpit. The Cairns produced by the Colemans, and later Mrs. Hutchinson, have added to the beauty and quality of Cairns from coast to coast. More than 60 of the 100 plus champions bred or owned by Wolfpit can trace their pedigrees back to that first bitch.

Line breeding became important in the Wolfpit kennels in the 1950s. This practice of breeding relatives to each other, such as a cousin to a cousin or a granddaughter to her grandfather, was not common at that time.

Ch. Caledonian Berry of Wolfpit, a recent multiple Best in Show dog. Breeder-owner-handled by Lydia C. Hutchinson.

This proved to be quite successful and, coupled with an occasional outcross, established a "look" that has carried on through generations. Top producing sires at Wolfpit include Ch. Cairnwoods Quince, Ch. Vinovium Caius, bred by Mrs. Summers in England, Ch. Persimmon of Wolfpit, and Ch.

Ch. Persimmon of Wolfpit. 1977 C.T.C.A. Best in Sweepstakes under judge and long-time breeder Helen Hunt.

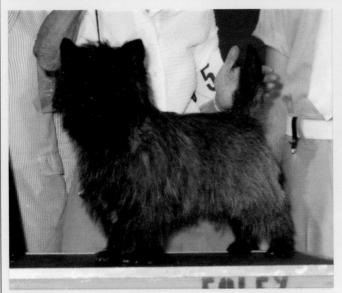

Ch. Cairnwoods Quince winning a Best in Show at five years of age. Owned by Mr. And Mrs. Taylor Coleman.

Ch. Cairndania Foxglove's Adelaide, Ch. Lofthouse Veleta, and Ch. Craiglyn Christmas Carol, a half-sister to Caius. Wolfpit has also produced its share of competitive show ring champions including their most current multiple specialty and best in show winner, Ch. Caledonian Berry of Wolfpit.

It is Quince, however, who is probably the most remembered dog to be owned and used at stud by Wolfpit and others. Quince figures prominently in modern pedigrees. His sons and daughters can be

Gadget's Gimmick of Wolfpit who was still siring winning offspring when he died in 1992. Important bitches in the program included

Ch. Cairmar Fancy Dresser in 1991. Tied with Quince as a top producer in breed history.

Ch. Bramblewood's Kit Kat, Fancy Dresser's 51st champion shown here a few days before her eighth birthday.

found in the pedigrees of Kim-E-Cairns, Pennylane, Nightfalls, Haverford, Rockwell, Crag Valley, Kamidon, Meriwynd, Wildwood, Cairmar, Braemar, Waterford, Kishorn, and many more. His dominance seems to carry itself on to future top producers as well.

Quince's great-grandson, Ch. Cairmar Fancy Dresser, joined him as all-time top producer in 1994 when his eight-year-old daughter Bramblewood's Kit Kat got off the couch and into the ring for the first time since she was a puppy and finished her championship. It is a mark of both sires that their get hold together well into their later years. An example is Ch. Whetstone Halston; a national specialty winner from the veterans class and a Fancy Dresser son. Bred by Joe and Betty Marcum of Cairmar, and owned by Glenna Barnes of Cairland, Fancy Dresser was sired by the Quince grandson Ch. Dapper Dan of Wildwood bred to Ch. Cairmar Fancy That. "Danny" had two all-breed Best in Shows, a Specialty Best, and numerous breed wins and group placements. One of his sons, Ch. Terriwood's Best Dressed, became a Best In Show winner himself in 1991 owner-handled at the Portland benched show. His littermate, Ch. Terriwood's Artful Dresser, won a Best in Show in Canada owner-handled in 1993. Only time will tell if Fancy Dresser's current winning sons and daughters will become top producers themselves.

Fancy Dresser's influence is still directly felt through sons and

daughters in the lines of Cairmar, Cairland, Whetstone, McLin, Criscairn, Pattwos, Raelain, Karen's, Fillkatom's, Bramblewood, and Terriwood, to name a few. Through grandsons and granddaughters he is behind some of the Cairns of Chasands, Copperglen, Morihas, Concannon, Highland, DeRan, Het's, Kilkeddan's, and Kishorn's.

Fancy Dresser's most prominent son was Ch. Whetstone Halston, bred by Molly Wilder and himself a top producer. Halston's dam was a top producing bitch, Ch. Cairmar Connecticut Yankee, whose sons and grandsons have won over half a dozen specialty best in shows. Halston, or Dirk as

Top left:*Ch. Whetstone Halston,* a C.T.C.A. Best of Breed winner shown here as a young dog. Middle left: **Ch. Cairmar Connecticut Yankee,** a top producing bitch who was also successful in the ring. Bottom left:**Ch. Whetstone Miss Dior,** sister to Ch. Whetstone Halston. Below:**Ch. Caithness Barnabas** out of Kamidon Country Squire x Ch. Caithness Rosalie.

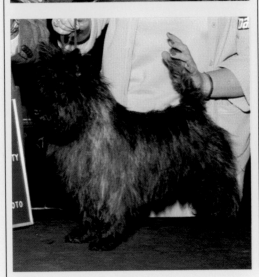

Ch. Cairmar Fancy That, dam of top producer Ch. Cairmar Fancy Dresser.

he was fondly called, was the 1986 Cairn Terrier Club of America national specialty winner, coming out of the veterans class.

Another top producer from this line is a Halston son, Ch. Cairmar Scot Free. Scottie has produced well over thirty champions with many in the ring today still on their way. One of his sons, Ch. Ollie North of the Highlands, was the Cairn Terrier Club of America's national specialty winner in 1989, following his Best in Sweeps at the national in 1988. Many other Scot Free offspring have done well at regional specialties.

All of this brings us to another kennel important in the history of the Cairn Terrier in North America. Although getting started later than either Cairndania or Wolfpit, the Cairmar Cairn Terriers of Betty and Joe Marcum have made their presence felt in every part of the country.

The Marcums first learned about Cairns when they saw a puppy bred by Mildred Bryant, now a judge of many breeds, but then a fancier of Cairn Terriers and Poodles. Later they were able to acquire one of their foundation Cairns from Mrs. Bryant, Ch.

49

Ch. Sharolaine's Kalypso was Best of Opposite Sex at C.T.C.A. in 1987.

the dam of Ch. Cairmar Fancy Dresser.

Another fortuitous breeding soon to follow was that of Killarney to Ch. Cairnwoods Quince. The result gave us Ch. Cairmar Connecticut Yankee, who produced four champions in her first litter out of Fancy Dresser, including Ch. Whetstone Halston, Ch.Whetstone Miss Dior, Ch. Whetstone Annie Hall and Ch. Cairmar Coco Chanel. Cindy went on to produce four more champions out of two other studs.

Meanwhile, the Barnabas offspring were bred to Ch. Tradorohg's Dunstan Claymore, CDX, a national specialty winner in 1975. Ginny Cadwallader's Ch. DeWinter's Duncan was also used to compliment this second line being developed by Cairmar. Duncan, another all-time top producer with over 20 champion get, bred to Cairmar Chandra Te produced Ch. Cairmar Call to Arms, another all-breed, owner-handled Best in Show winner. Charger in turn produced, among others, Ch. Cairmar Kitten on the Keys, who established a dynasty of her own with her many champion offspring.

Tradorohg's Connamarah, who was the dam of twelve champions for them. Also acquired in those early years were Ch. Milbryan Killarney O'Cairmar, Ch. Caithness Periwinkle, and Ch. Caithness Barnabas. The latter two were made available by Mrs. Betty Stone. Barnabas stands as one of the top producers of all time with 33 champion offspring. His influence was felt mostly by Cairmar and the Lakewood kennel of Nell Stumph, although he sired champions for Metcourt, Gamac, Chriscay, and Dapper Cairns as well. Periwinkle bred to Mildred Bryant's Ch. Caithness Colonel produced Ch. Cairmar Colonel Peri and Ch. Cairmar Fancy That,

Deciding to obtain outcross stock, the Marcums imported two bitches from England, Am. Ch. Greetavale Golden Vow of Courtrai and Avenelhouse Plain Jane. These two bitches in particular are found in many Cairmar pedigrees and are behind current top winners and producers.

All told, Cairmar has produced over 100 champions. Counted among them are Ch. Cairmar Cowardly Lion, a multiple Best in Show winner in recent years and one of the top winners of all time, the previously mentioned top winners and producers, and others such as Ch. Cairmar Bobby McLin, Ch. Cairmar Cachet, CD, Ch. Cairmar Andrew of Raelain, Ch. Cairmar Amy Amy Amy, Ch. Cairmar Infernal Angel, Ch. Cairmar Stormy Dawn, Ch. Cairmar Miss Chance, Ch. Cairmar Private Collection, and Ch. Cairmar Critic's Choice. Cairmar dogs and bitches will be found in the pedigrees of Whetstone, Cairland, Brehannon, Glenmore, Copperglen, Rutherglen, DeRan, Raelain, McLin, Wildwood, LinCairn, Bramblewood, Terriwood, Craigcastle, Redcoat, Chesapeake, Spring Valle, Tanglevine, Pennylane, Muf-N-Den, Karengary, and Highlands, among others.

A top producer today who at the relatively young age of nine is still siring Best In Show and Specialty winners is Ch. Sharolaine's Kalypso. Bred by Elaine Eschbach

Ch. Cairmar Bobby McLin, *sire of Ch. Cairmar Cowardly Lion, a multiple Best in Show winner.*

and owned by Elaine and Cairndania's Betty Hyslop, "Lippy" has produced 33 champions to date. His influence was at first felt mainly in the mid-west, but has spread throughout the United States and Canada as the quality of his get has made itself known. His son Ch. Foxairn Tinman, bred and exhibited by Sanderson and Margaret McIlwain, has multiple Best and Specialty Bests to his

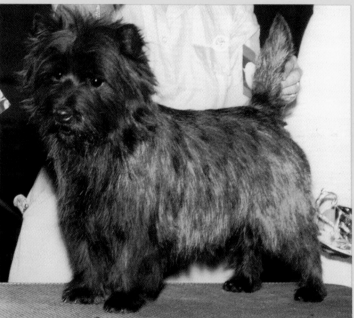

Ch. Gadget's Gimmick of Wolfpit was Best of Opposite Sex at C.T.C.A. in 1985.

credit. Tinman is also making his mark as a sire. Of course, there are certainly many other top producers of note in the history of the breed. Ch. Gayla Cairn's Davey, bred and owned by Nancy Thompson, produced 30 champions, all but one of them for Gayla Cairns. In fact, Davey and Ch. Kenmure's Felicity produced

ten champions together, while Gayla Cairn's Maggie bred to him produced seven. Ch. Gayla Cairn's Gregor McKim and Ch. Gayla Cairn's Inspiration both produced several champions for Mrs. Thompson.

Other strong producers include Ch. Moonbeam of Redletter who produced 19 Lakewood champions for Nell Stumph, Ch. Wyesider Grey Knight with 17 champion get for Cairnwoods, Bagpipe, Woodmist, Caithness, Kamidon's, Pipers, Justcairn, the Grey Knight son Ch. Cairnwoods Fiver who produced 14 champions in the kennels of Cairnwoods, the Abhalter's Coralrocks Cairns, Whetstone, Albanoch, Cairnlogs, and Wildwood. Also producing 15 champions were Ch. Caithness Colonel, Ch. Heathcairn Cuthbert, Ch. Gayla Cairn's Gregor McKim and Ch. Redletter McBrigand.

Not to be forgotten are the bitches who have produced well. The top producing bitch in the United States with 22 champions is Ch. Gayla Cairn's Nora. All of these champions came from only four sires, all Gayla Cairns dogs. Another Gayla Cairn bitch is Ch. Gayla Cairn's Hope with 11 champions. Ch. Kenmure's Felicity was the dam of ten Gayla Cairn champions.

Other top producing bitches were Ginger Mist of Merriwood who produced over 15 Lakewood champions, Ch. Tradorohg's Connamarah already mentioned as a Cairmar foundation dam, Ch. Lakewood's Foxy Lady with ten champions for Lakewood's, Ch. GlenCairn Molly McNeill with nine champions, all GlenCairn and eight of them by Ch. Craigly Jamie McFlair, Ch. Hillston Geraldine and Cairndania Clansman's Holifax with nine and seven champion get respectively for Cairndania. Kim-E-Cairn's My Choice had nine champions for the Kim-E-Cairn kennel. Ch. Bayberry of Wolfpit produced eight champions out of MacBrian, Persimmon, and Gadget's Gimmick of Wolfpit. Shadow's Sterling Silver produced seven champions for Cairland, all out of Ch. Cairmar Fancy Dresser. And Ch. Col-Cairn's Ruffy Righinn has produced many champions for the Hickey's at Tigh Terrie's Cairns. Each passing year adds new names to these top producing lists and updates will need to be made periodically.

Top winners are important

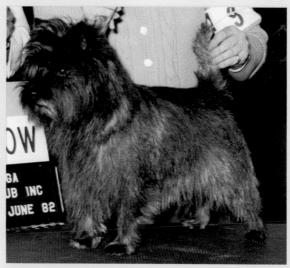

AmCan. Ch. Foxgrove Jeronimo, a two-time C.T.C.A. Best of Breed winner and a multiple Best in Show winner. Owner, Betty Hyslop.

too. Of special note are the Cairn Terrier Club of America national specialty winners. This show is where breeders and exhibitors come to show the best of the best to the judges and to other breeders. To win Best of Breed at

AmCan. Ch. Foxgrove Jessica, winning the C.T.C.A. Best of Opposite in 1982. Owned by Betty Hyslop.

the national is the highest honor that can be bestowed upon a Cairn and his or her owner, breeder, and handler. Even a placement in the classes at this show, where the competition is friendly but fierce, is to be cherished. Winners since 1980 include Ch. Cairnwoods Quince, previously mentioned as a four-time winner of the national. Best of Opposite Sex to him in 1980 was Ch. Foxy Loxy Vixen of Haverford.

In 1981 and again in 1982 the Best of Breed winner was Ch. Foxgrove Jeronimo, one of the important sires imported by Betty Hyslop of Cairndania. The Best of Opposite Sex in 1981 was Ch. MacBriar of Wolfpit. Best of Opposite Sex to Jeronimo in 1982 was Ch. Foxgrove Jessica. Foxgrove imports have proven their worth at other nationals as well, with Ch. Foxgrove Jester winning in 1976 and Ch. Foxgrove Susanella, a bitch, winning in 1974.

In 1983 the national specialty was won by Ch. Chasands Yankee Peddler with Best of Opposite honors going to Ch. Whetstone Fair N' Warmer. Ch. Cairnlea's Robson topped the breed in 1984. Best of Opposite Sex that year was Ch. Cairnhoe Carronade.

The next year, 1985, provided a

Top left:**Ch. Copperglen Fame N Fortune,** national specialty winner in 1987. Middle left:**Ch. Buccaneers Iris At Terratote,** a National Specialty winner from the classes. Below left:**Ch. Copperglen Foxtrot,** a multiple regional specialty winner.

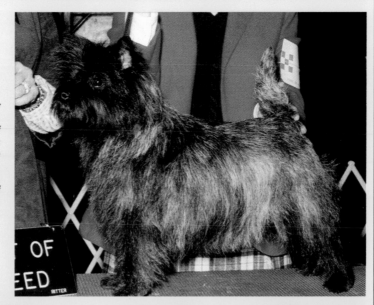

Right:*Ch. Whetstone Fair N' Warmer, CD,* a C.T.C.A. national specialty Best of Opposite Sex winner as well as an obedience title holder. Below:*Ch. Cairnhoe Carronade,* winning C.T.C.A. Best of Opposite Sex in 1984.

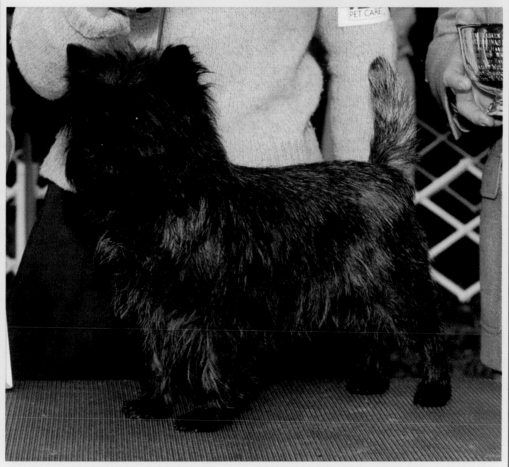

thrill for breeder/owner/handler Elfie Payne when her Bred–By-Exhibitor class bitch Ch. Buccaneer's Iris at Terratote went from Winners Bitch on to Best of Breed. Best of Opposite Sex went to Ch. Gadget's Gimmick of Wolfpit.

1986 was the year of the veteran with Ch. Whetstone Halston taking the breed from the Veteran Dog class. Best of Opposite Sex was Ch. Copperglen Fame N Fortune, who went on in 1987 to win Best of Breed herself. Best of Opposite to her was Ch. Sharolaine's Kalypso. These two have since been bred to each other and have produced a specialty and group winning bitch, Ch. Copperglen Foxtrot. This is but another example of the axiom that breeding high quality

Top left:**Ch. Reanda's Britta at Redcoat** *winning Best of Opposite at the 1991 C.T.C.A. roving national specialty. Owned by Redcoat Cairns.* Middle left:**Ch. Nightfalls Encore,** *a three time Best of Opposite Sex winner at the C.T.C.A. national specialty.* Bottom left:**Ch. Ollie North of the Highlands** *winning C.T.C.A. Best of Breed in 1989.* Below:**Ch. Lydia's Britt Harmony** *winning C.T.C.A. Best of Opposite in 1988.*

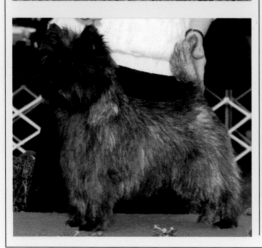

dogs to each other is the best way to produce top quality.

Ch. Tidewater Master Gold, the top winning Cairn Terrier in the United States with 15 all-breed Best in Show wins and a group win at Westminster, also won the national specialty in 1988. Best of Opposite Sex went to Ch.

Ch. Goosedown's Tailor Made, a three-time national specialty winner.

Lydia's Britt Harmony.

At the C.T.C.A. Sweepstakes in 1988, Ch. Ollie North of the Highlands went Best in Sweeps, a prelude to his Best of Breed win at the national specialty in 1989. Best of Opposite that year was Ch. Nightfalls Encore, a young bitch destined to keep winning.

Ch. Goosedown's Tailor Made won Best of Breed in 1990, again at the first roving national specialty in June of 1991, and yet again at the national at Montgomery County in 1991. This young dog is already making his mark as a sire with several champion get. At both the 1990 and 1991 Pennsylvania specialty shows, Ch. Nightfalls Encore was

Best of Opposite, retiring the Ch. Redletter Miss Splinters trophy as a three-time winner. At the roving specialty, Ch. Reanda's Britta at Redcoat was Best of Opposite Sex. At the 1992 national specialty, Ch. Glenarden's Debut Attraction, a granddaughter of 1987's Best of Breed winner Ch. Copperglen Fame N Fortune, won the breed. She had been Winners Bitch in 1991 at the ripe old age of six months and a few days—at her first show! Best of Opposite was Ch. Ohioville Rooster. The roving national specialty, usually held every other year, was hosted by the Chicago Suburban Cairn Terrier Club in June of 1993. Best of Breed went to Ch. Sharolaine's

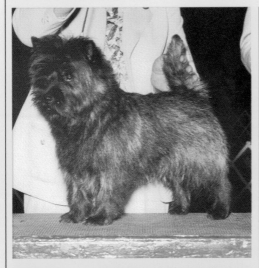

Top left:***Ch. Chasand's Yankee Peddler*** *won Best of Breed at the C.T.C.A. national specialty in 1983. Out of Ch. Cairmar Critics Choice x Chasand's Raggedy Ann. Owners, Charles and Sandra LeClair.* Middle left:***Ch. Cairnlea's Robson,*** *C.T.C.A. Best of Breed winner in 1984. Owners, Sanderson and Margaret McIlwaine.* Bottom left:***Ch. Cairmar Kitten On The Keys*** *is a Call To Arms daughter and a top producing bitch. Owned by Betty Marcum.* Top right:***Ch. Cairmar Call To Arms,*** *a Best in Show winner, breeder-owner-handled by Betty Marcum.*

Kingdom Kome and Best of Opposite went to Ch. Tigh Terrie's Hello Dolly.

At the regular national held in Montgomery in 1993, Best of Breed honors went to Ch. Tigh Terrie's Hello Dolly, daughter of three-time national winner Ch. Goosedown's Tailor Made. Ch. Caledonian Berry of Wolfpit was Best of Opposite. Both of these Cairns are All-breed Best In Show winners as well. Always remember when looking at show records that being a top winner does not guarantee a dog to be a top producer. While some big winners can put their stamp on the breed, when planning a breeding program it is usually advisable to look toward the consistent producers rather than just the current show ring winners.

Right:*Ch. Bonnie Vamp of Wolfpit* out of Ch. Cairnwoods Quince x Ch. Bonnie Vixen of Wolfpit owned by Lydia Coleman Hutchinson. Below:*Ch. Cairmar Cowardly Lion,* a multiple Best in Show winner owned by Betty Marcum.

59

Left: *Ch. Gaelic Haggis MacBasher* owned by Betty Hyslop. Above right: *AmCan. Ch. Cairndania Sam's Sundew,* a Canadian Best in Show winner and two-time Best of Breed winner at Westminster. Owned by Betty Hyslop. Below: *Ch. Foxgrove Susanella* won Best of Breed both at Crufts and Westminster in the mid-1970s.

Above: ***Ch. Sharolaine's Kalypso*** owned by Betty Hyslop. Below: ***AmCan. Ch. Wee Gaelic Todd Cairndania*** owned by Betty Hyslop.

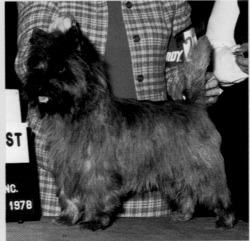

Top left:***Ch. Foxgrove Jester,*** *winning C.T.C.A. Best of Breed in 1976.* Middle left:***Ch. Quince's Spunky of Wolfpit*** *at age 15. Quince's first champion.* Bottom left: ***Ch. Avenelhouse Plain Jane,*** *an English import brought over by Cairmar and found in many Cairmar pedigrees.* Top right: ***AmCan. Ch. Rogerlyn Sea Hawk Salty Sam,*** *1978 C.T.C.A. Best of Breed winner.*

Top left: **AmCan. Ch. Cairndania Brigrey Berry Red,** *1977 C.T.C.A. Best of Opposite Sex winner.* Top right: **Ch. Foxgrove Mutt,** *an important English import who won the Veteran class at the C.T.C.A. national specialty in 1989.* Below: **AmCan. Ch. Foxairn Tinman,** *a multiple Best in Show winner who has won the breed over 200 times, including Westminster Kennel Club 1993 and 1994. Owner, Betty Hyslop.*

Ch. Uniquecottage Georgie Girl. *A beautiful head study of a modern English import bitch. Owned by Pauli Christy. Photo courtesy of "Moments by Jane."*

The Standard in Great Britain

Just as a builder needs a written plan or blueprints to follow when constructing a new house, each breed of dog needs a written guideline for breeders and judges to follow. This guideline is called a standard. Every parent club puts together a standard, a written description of the ideal dog of that breed, and submits it to a national organization, such as The Kennel Club in Great Britain or the American Kennel Club in the U.S., for approval and acceptance. This standard becomes the blueprint and foundation for the breed. It is imperative that breeders, exhibitors, and judges understand it thoroughly in order to keep the breed type correct over the years.

The first standard, described as the show points, was composed in October, 1911, shortly after the Cairn Terrier started to be exhibited at shows. Among those present were Mr. Allan MacDonald of Waternish, Mrs. Alastair Campbell, the Lady Sophie Scott, Lady Charles Bentinck, the Hon. Mary Hawke, Mrs. Fleming, and Florence M. Ross. If discussions on breed type today are any indication of what went on then, the input from various breeders was surely interesting if not downright heated. Even then, each Cairn fancier had his or her own ideas of what constituted breed type and quality. Their ability to reach an agreement and get it in writing is a tribute to their dedication to the breed.

It is interesting to follow the changes in the standard over the years. The main points seem to appear in every version, but some other considerations which seemed important to the authors at the time have disappeared altogether or have been changed in wording, perhaps to allow more leeway in interpretation. For example, the first show points were as follows (italics mine):

GENERAL APPEARANCE (20) Small, active, game; very hardy in appearance; strong, though compactly built. Should stand well forward on fore-paws, strong quarters, deep in ribs; very free in movement; coat hard enough to resist rain; head small, but in proportion to body. *A general foxy appearance is the chief characteristic of this Working Terrier.*

SKULL (10) Broad in proportion; strong, but not too long or heavy jaw. *A slight indentation between eyes*; hair should be rather full on top of head.

Toptwig Wideawake bred by Gay Marsh and owned by Lynne Nabors.

MUZZLE (10) Powerful, but not heavy; very strong jaw, with large teeth; *roof of mouth black.*

EYES (5) Set wide apart, *large,* hazel or dark hazel, rather sunk, with shaggy eyebrows.

EARS (5) Small, pointed, well carried, and erect, but not too closely set.

TAIL (5) *About 6 inches,* well furnished with hair, but not feathery; carried gaily, but must not curl over back.

BODY (25) Compact, straight back, deep ribs, strong sinews, hindquarters very strong.

LEGS AND FEET (10) *Low in leg;* good, but not too large bone; fore-legs should not be out at elbows, but fore-feet may be slightly turned out; fore-feet larger than hind; legs must be covered with hard hair; *pads should be black.*

COAT (20) Coat hard, but not coarse, with good undercoat and head well furnished; in colour – sandy, grey, brindles, or nearly black. Dark points, such as ears, muzzle, very typical.

Note the words in italics, some of which have been completely eliminated from modern adaptations of the standard. Nowadays, no mention is made of the roof of the mouth or the pads of the feet being black, although there is reference to lack of pigmentation as a fault. In current standards, in both the U.S. and Great Britain, no absolute length of tail is set out, although a long tail is considered quite unattractive. The direction that the dogs should be "low on leg" is now more often than not considered a fault, depending upon how low "low on leg" actually is.

The desire for an indentation between the eyes is now described as a decided stop in the American standard. Novices listening to breeders who have been around for many years will sometimes hear them say something about the need for an indentation between the eyes or they will see a judge press his or her thumb against the stop during the judging. Knowing that a decided stop is necessary from the current standard, the newcomers are apt to wonder why an indentation is also required. Obviously this is a holdover from the original standard that many feel is still important to breed type. The

British standard still mentions this requirement.

The requirement of "a generally foxy appearance" has caused much confusion over the years. A close examination and comparison of the fox and the Cairn Terrier show some similarities, such as a strong jaw and pricked ears, but the fox has a snipey look to it which is incorrect in the Cairn. Perhaps the original wording was meant as a description of the distinct first impression of the Cairn, the sharp eye with its devilish sparkle and keenness of expression, the quickness of movement and litheness of the hunter. It should certainly never be mistaken to mean that a Cairn should have

Above: **Sybster Spellbinder,** a Scottish Cairn from Dundee. Owned by Mrs. Sybil Berrecloth. Below: **Harlight Hellion** at 11 months of age. Owner, Mrs. L.Z. Spence.

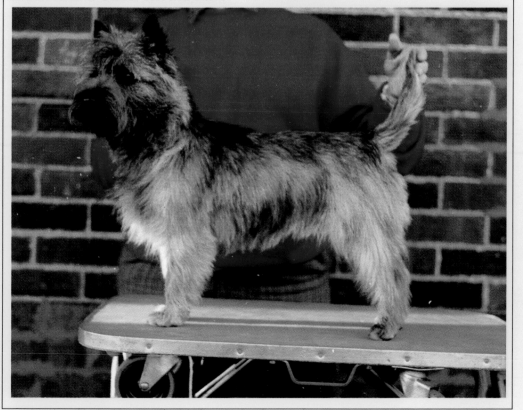

Ch. Uniquecottage Georgie Girl, an English bitch imported to the U.S., at two years of age. Owner, Pauli Christy.

the more narrow skull of the fox or its longer body and bushy tail.

In 1922 a revised standard was written wherein some points of the first standard were dropped and others clarified. Under the heading "General Appearance" the word "shaggy" was introduced. The description of the eyes was changed from large to medium, a small change that surely incurred much debate before being added since the size and shape of the eye is so important to a proper Cairn expression. All mention of black on the roof of the mouth and pads of the feet was eliminated. However, the addition of thin or ferrety feet as a fault was interjected. Medium length of back was added, probably to offset the rather longer backs seen in many dogs of the day. Now, as it was then, the word medium is subject to interpretation.

It is interesting to note that an addition to the 1922 standard stated, "In order to keep this breed to the best old working type, any cross with a modern Scottish Terrier will be considered objectionable." However, crossing a Cairn Terrier and a West Highland White Terrier was an accepted practice until litters of such matings were banned from registration in 1925 in Great Britain, following the edict by the American Kennel Club earlier in the United States. According to some breed historians, most notably T.W.L. Caspersz in his book *The Cairn Terrier Handbook,* the requirement to stay away from the Scottish Terrier was the result of some breeders crossing Scotties and Westies to obtain white puppies, which were popular at that time. Brindles from these litters were sold as Cairn Terriers. While they were obviously terriers, they certainly were not Cairn

Terriers.

While other revisions were made after 1922, in 1982 the standard in Great Britain was revised for the final time. Still, it varied little in essence from the preceding standards. The allowance for size was increased slightly and clarified with height and weight descriptions. Rather than a scale of points for faults, a more general statement of guidance was given. Of great importance, especially to those across the ocean who imported dogs for show and stud purposes, a note was added that males should have both testicles descended into the scrotum. The American Kennel Club has always stressed the importance of normal descended testicles. Dogs which were affected with monorchidism or cryptorchidism were not and are still not allowed to be exhibited in conformation.

THE CAIRN TERRIER BREED STANDARD ADOPTED IN GREAT BRITAIN IN 1982

General Appearance

Agile, alert, of workmanlike, natural appearance. Standing well

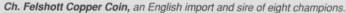

Ch. Felshott Copper Coin, an English import and sire of eight champions.

Sybster Sepia at 14 years of age. Owner, Mrs. Sybil Berrecloth.

dark hazel. Slightly sunk with shaggy eyebrows.

Ears

Small, pointed, well carried and erect, not too closely set nor heavily coated.

Mouth

Large teeth. Jaws strong with perfect, regular and complete scissor bite, i.e. upper teeth closely overlapping lower teeth and set square to the jaws.

Neck

Well set on, not short.

Forequarters

Sloping shoulders, medium length of leg, good but not too heavy bone. Forelegs never out at elbow. Legs covered with harsh hair.

Body

Back level, medium length. Well sprung deep ribs; strong supple loin.

Hindquarters

Very strong muscular thighs. Good, but not excessive, bend of stifle. Hocks well let down, inclining neither in nor out when viewed from the rear.

forward on forepaws. Strong quarters. Deep in rib, very free movement. Weather-resistant coat.

Characteristics

Should impress as being active, game and hardy.

Temperament

Fearless and gay disposition; assertive but not aggressive.

Head & Skull

Head small, but in proportion to body. Skull broad; decided indentation between the eyes with a definite stop. Muzzle powerful, jaw strong but not long or heavy. Nose black. Head well furnished.

Eyes

Wide apart, medium in size,

Feet

Forefeet, larger than hind, may be slightly turned out. Pads thick and strong. Thin, narrow or spreading feet and long nails objectionable.

Tail

Short, balanced, well furnished with hair but not feathery. Neither high nor low set, carried gaily but not turned down towards back.

Gait/Movement

Very free-flowing stride. Forelegs reaching well forward. Hind legs giving strong propulsion. Hocks neither too close nor too wide.

Above: *Harlight Honeybunch,* owned by Mrs. L.Z. Spence. Below:*Three Scottish Cairns:* **Sybster Desmond, Duncan,** and **Skipper,** owned by Mrs. Sybil Berrecloth.

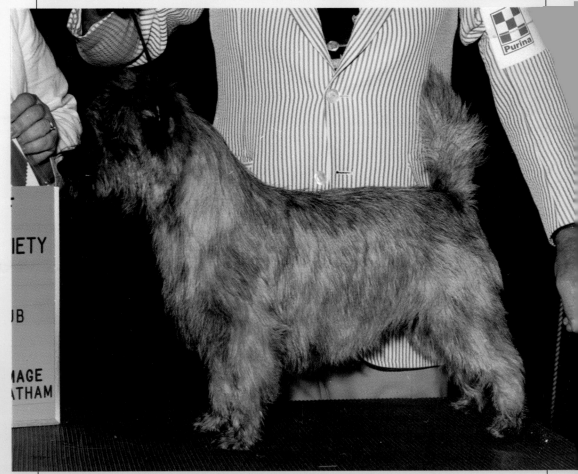

Ch. Pinetop Paperchase, an English import to the U.S. owned by Susan and Jack De Witt. Photo by Charles Tatham.

Coat

Very important. Weather-resistant. Must be double-coated, with profuse, harsh, but not coarse, outer coat; undercoat short, soft and close. Open coats objectionable. Slight wave permissible.

Colour

Cream wheaten, red, grey or nearly black. Brindling in all these colours acceptable. Not solid back, or white, or black and tan. Dark points, such as ears and muzzle, very typical.

Size

Approximately 28-31 cms (11-12 ins) at withers, but in proportion to weight-ideally 6-7.5 kgs (14-16 lbs).

Faults

Any departure from the foregoing points should be considered a fault and the seriousness with which the fault should be regarded should be in exact proportion to its degree.

NOTE: Male animals should have two apparently normal testicles fully descended into the scrotum.

The official standard of the Cairn Terrier in the United States, much as the preceding British standard, goes into some detail about the structure, temperament, and other physical attributes of the breed. Breeders in both countries essentially want the same things in their Cairns. The dogs of Great Britain are allowed to be somewhat

larger, 11 to 12 inches in height as opposed to the recommended 10 inches for a dog in the United States. In fact, many breeders speak of two "types" of Cairns, the British type and the American type.

Right: Three **Harlight** champions: **Henry, Hornblower, and Hello Honey** owned by Mrs. L.Z. Spence. *Below:* Four-month-old Scottish puppies owned by Mrs. Sybil Berrecloth. Ears occasionally can take five to six months to stand fully erect, although four months is more common.

AmCan. Ch. Foxgrove Jester. *U.S. Best in Show winner imported from England by Betty Hyslop.*

The American Standard and Amplification

Cairn Terriers were imported to the United States early in their history as a distinct breed. The Cairn Terrier Club of America was accepted into the American Kennel Club in 1917, giving the breed solid recognition. Fanciers continued to import dogs from Great Britain while they bred their own lines in the States. For many years the British dogs competing and finishing championships in the United States outnumbered the American dogs.

It was natural that the first standard in the United States was quite similar to the British standard. It is interesting that this standard had two disqualifications, one being a flesh-colored nose and the other being dogs weighing more than 15 or (except puppies) less than 12 pounds. Bitches weighing more than 14, or (except puppies) less than 11 pounds were also to be disqualified. By 1917, the American Kennel Club also stated that the color white was not allowed.

The current official breed standard for the Cairn Terrier in the United States was approved by the American Kennel Club on

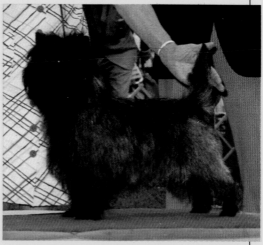

Top-producer and multiple national specialty winner **Ch. Cairnwoods Quince** *in his prime at six years of age.*

May 10 , 1938. Although there have been movements at times to make changes, the standard has thus far survived intact. The American Kennel Club is currently requesting breed clubs to rewrite their standards on a voluntary basis using a specific format and terminology approved by the AKC. This is an attempt to standardize all breed standards, apparently so that they can be better understood by those unfamiliar with the breed. However, many believe that much of the flavor and character expressed in the current standard would be lost if terms used for years were to be dropped in favor of more generic terms.

THE OFFICIAL AMERICAN BREED STANDARD OF THE CAIRN TERRIER

General Appearance

That of an active, game, hardy, small working terrier of the short-legged class; very free in its movements, strongly but not heavily built, standing well forward on its forelegs, deep in the ribs, well coupled with strong hindquarters and presenting a well-proportioned build with a medium length of back, having a hard, weather-resisting coat; head shorter and wider than any other terrier and well furnished with hair giving a general foxy expression.

Skull

Broad in proportion to length with a decided stop and well furnished with hair on the top of the head, which may be somewhat softer than the body coat. *Muzzle* Strong but not too long or heavy. *Teeth* Large –mouth neither overshot nor undershot. *Nose* Black. *Eyes* Set wide apart,

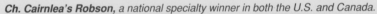

Ch. Cairnlea's Robson, a national specialty winner in both the U.S. and Canada.

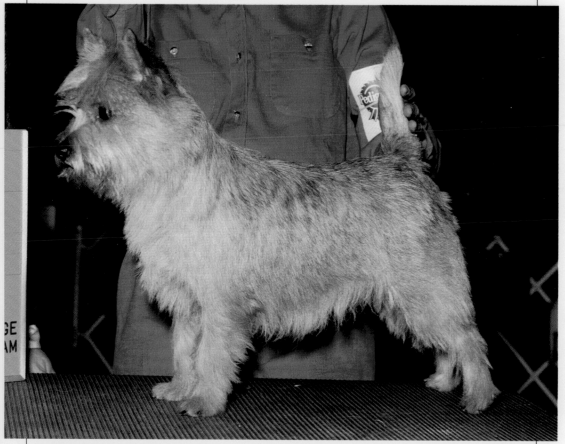

Ch. Happicairn Pinetopper, a striking red Cairn out of English stock. Owned by Susan and Jack De Witt. Photo by Chuck Tatham.

rather sunken, with shaggy eyebrows, medium in size, hazel or dark hazel in color, depending on body color, with a keen terrier expression. *Ears* Small, pointed, well carried erectly, set wide apart on the side of the head. Free from long hairs.

Tail

In proportion to head, well furnished with hair but not feathery. Carried gaily but must not curl over back. Set on at back level.

Body

Well muscled, strong, active body with well-sprung, deep ribs, coupled to strong hindquarters, with a level back of medium length, giving an impression of strength and activity without heaviness.

Shoulders, Legs and Feet

A sloping shoulder, medium length of leg, good but not too heavy bone; forelegs should not be out at elbows, and be perfectly straight, but forefeet may be slightly turned out. Forefeet larger

Ch. Terriwood's Lasting Legacy, a Canadian Best in Specialty winning bitch. Photo by Animal World Studio.

than hindfeet. Legs must be covered with hard hair. Pads should be thick and strong and dog should stand well up on its feet.

Coat
Hard and weather resistant.

Ch. MacBriar of Wolfpit at one year of age. Owner, Lydia C. Hutchinson.

Must be double-coated with profuse harsh outer coat and short, soft, close furry undercoat.

Color
May be of any color except white. Dark ears, muzzle and tail tip are desirable.

Ideal Size
Involves the weight, the height at the withers and the length of body. Weight for bitches, 13 pounds, for dogs, 14 pounds. Height at the withers—bitches, $9^1/_2$ inches, dogs, 10 inches. Length of body from $14^1/_4$ to 15 inches from the front of the chest to back of hindquarters. The dog must be of balanced proportions and appear neither leggy nor too low to ground; and neither too short nor too long in body. Weight and measurements are for matured dogs at two years of age. Older dogs may weigh slightly in excess and growing dogs may be under these weights and measurements.

Condition
Dogs should be shown in good hard flesh, well muscled, and neither too fat or thin. Should be in full good coat with plenty of head furnishings, be clean, combed, brushed and tidied up on ears, tail, feet and general outline. Should move freely and easily on a loose lead, should not cringe on being

handled, should stand up on their toes and show marked terrier characteristics.

Faults

1. SKULL Too narrow in skull.

2. MUZZLE Too long and heavy a foreface; mouth overshot or undershot.

3. EYES Too large, prominent, yellow, and ringed are all objectionable.

4. EARS Too large, round at points, set too close together, set too high on the head; heavily covered with hair.

5. LEGS AND FEET Too light or too heavy bone. Crooked forelegs or out at elbow. Thin, ferrety feet; feet let down on the heel or too open and spread. Too high or too low on the leg.

6. BODY Too short back and compact a body, hampering quickness of movement and turning ability. Too long, weedy and snaky a body, giving an

Three-time national specialty winner **Ch. Goosedown's Tailor Made.** Photo by Holloway.

impression of weakness. Tail set on too low. Back not level.

7. COAT Open coats, blousy coats, too short or dead coats, lack of sufficient undercoat, lack of head furnishings, lack of hard hair on the legs. Silkiness or curliness. A slight wave permissible.

8. NOSE Flesh or light-colored nose.

9.COLOR White on chest, feet or other parts of body.

Approved May 10, 1938
American Kennel Club

AMPLIFICATION OF THE STANDARD

Now that we have the standard, how do we relate it to the dog? If a newcomer to Cairns were to read the standard without ever laying eyes on an actual specimen, he would still have little clue as to how a Cairn Terrier should look. He would know it would be a smallish fellow with pricked ears, four legs, and a tail, but that

AmCan. Ch. Rogerlyn Sea Hawk's Salty Sam owned by Betty Hyslop.

would be about it. Even someone familiar with the breed must know how to relate the standard to the dog and his original purpose as a working terrier: to be able to go to ground in tunnels often only 8 or 9 inches in diameter to face the teeth of his quarry or bolt it out of the earth for the hunters to dispatch.

The Cairn Terrier Club of America has a booklet on the interpretation, clarification, and amplification of the Cairn Terrier Standard. It is "must" reading for those interested in exhibiting, breeding, or judging Cairns. This author will attempt to go even a bit farther in amplifying the standard, but it must be understood that the descriptions given are those of the author, complete with possible subjective interpretation. After all, interpreting and applying the standard are what breeding and judging are all about and no one can deny that these are quite subjective experiences.

Ch. Rogerlyn Sailor Cairndania owned by Glenna Barnes.

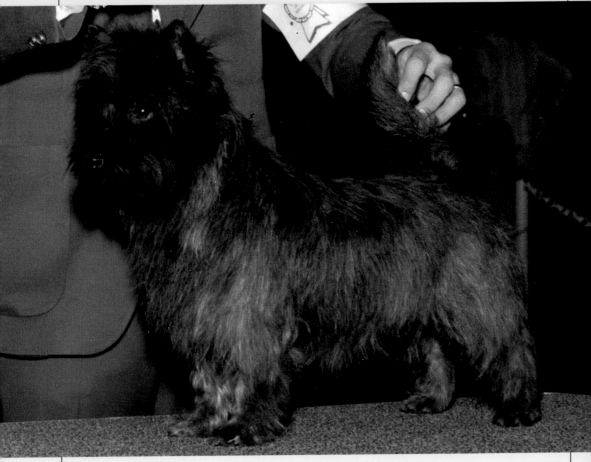

VARIATIONS IN TYPE

A note must be made here regarding the variations in type found in the Cairn Terrier. As you look at the pictures in this book, you will see that there is a great deal of difference in the appearance of the dogs. Even the national specialty winners pictured from past years vary in type. How can this be? Which one is correct?

When the Cairn first emerged as a distinct breed, his true origins were a mystery. Early

Ch. Cairnwood's Quince proving once again that really good dogs remain good, no matter what their age. In this picture Quince was eight years old and won the breed and the group in strong competition. Owners, Mr. and Mrs. Taylor Coleman.

breeders selected and bred a terrier which until then had been used strictly for hunting vermin. Each crofter bred his own dogs to his own needs and desires. Overall the dog was small and game with a medium length of back and leg, pricked ears and a varminty expression. However, due to the diverse gene pool, there was great variation in the general appearance or type. The pioneers who obtained dogs for their show kennels and worked to get the breed recognized as the Cairn Terrier also had their own opinions of what constituted type. A review of the early champions shows that they were often fairly dissimilar in the details of their appearance. Some were higher on leg, some were low. Some had longer tails, some had longer backs. Head shape and ear size were different. And yet, they were all obviously Cairn Terriers. Many of the books written by breeders from this time period talk freely of this type from kennel "A" and that type of Cairn from kennel "B." With the variation in type present from the very beginnings of the breed, it is no wonder that we have variations today.

So, what is type? The simplest way to define it is that which is typical to the breed. This includes overall shape or silhouette, size,

Ch. MacBriar of Wolfpit winning Best of Opposite Sex C.T.C.A. in 1981. Owner, Lydia C. Hutchinson. Photo by Martin Booth.

size. Type is more about the overall look of the dog which lets the observer know immediately that it is a Cairn Terrier, regardless of its variations.

Most often heard is the discussion of the "British" and "American" types. The "British type" is described as a larger dog, often higher on leg, and having a longer back than the "American type," which is smaller and often somewhat shorter in back. While these generalizations are for the most part true, it must be recognized that there are many more variations in type than just these two. The important thing is to realize that they are just that— variations. It is doubtful that the next time you go to a show you will hear the person next to you at ringside say, "Well, I certainly don't care for that variation of dog." We will have to understand that "type" is used as a catchall word and carry on accordingly.

We are still left with the

substance, and expression. For example, it is typical for a Cairn to have pricked ears rather than drop or rose ears. It is typical for a Cairn to stand approximately 10 inches high at the withers rather than 20 inches. It is typical for the outline of a Cairn to be quite different than that of a German Shepherd Dog.

Many people talk about variations in certain aspects of type as if that were type itself. "I don't care for that type of Cairn. He is too big." In reality, this comment is about size in relation to type, not about type itself. Or how about, "That judge doesn't like that type of dog. He has too narrow a head." This comment is about the variation of head proportions, not about overall type. While these comments might be valid to a certain degree, they condense type into just head or

Ch. Copperglen Sparrow Hawk, owned by the author.

problem of what is correct? Look again at the pictures in this book. They are all typical of the breed. They are obviously Cairn Terriers. However, they all vary in certain aspects. Some are larger, some are longer in back, some are higher or lower on leg. Ear size varies, as does length of tail and neck. Grooming makes some look different than others. Even the heads and expressions are different. So which one is correct? That answer lies in the eyes of the beholder and his own interpretation of the standard. Do we have a "problem" with varying types? Not as long as the dogs still look and act like Cairn Terriers according to the standard of the breed.

Right: ***Ch. Cairnhowse Starfire*** *out of Ch. Lakewood's Raisin Cane x Ch. Cairnhowse Morning Star. Owners, Jerry and Sharon Howse. Below:* ***AmCan. Ch. Foxgrove Susanella,*** *a C.T.C.A. Best of Breed and a Best in Show winner. Owner, Betty Hyslop.*

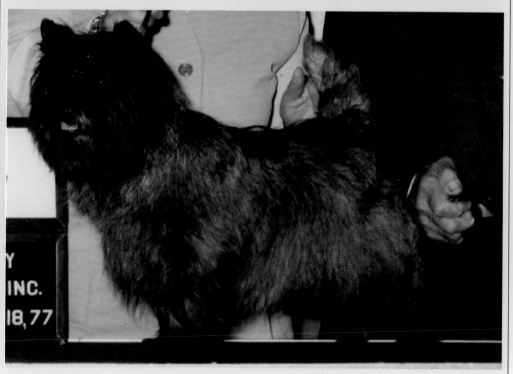

Bramblewood's Silver Lining is a cream-colored Cairn with dark points. Owned by the author.

Head to Toe:
An Interpretation of the Standard

THE HEAD

Many people consider the Cairn to be a "head" breed. This means that the proper headpiece and expression are extremely important to breed type. Unfortunately, this can also mean that the rest of the body is not given enough credence or importance when the dog is being judged. A beautiful head is not reason enough to ignore significant faults elsewhere.

The typical Cairn expression gives the immediate impression of a dog that is all terrier, a dog who will say "make me" when given a command. The overall head shape is somewhat rounded due to the thick coat, which stands naturally away from the skin. Small, dark ears whose tips stand just above the coat are pricked in interest at the slightest sound. Large or improperly set ears are to be penalized. A Cairn's ears are set a bit more to the side of the head than the Westie and certainly not on top of the skull as in the Scottie.

A fairly short muzzle holds teeth that are surprisingly large. The muzzle is not quite as long from nose to stop as the skull is from stop to occiput, or the high point of the skull between and just behind the ears. Dark eyes (but not black) sparkling with mischief and intelligence are set deep under a shaggy brow. The eyes are not round, nor are they almond shaped, but lie somewhere between the two. A large, round eye takes away from the keen expression necessary to the proper Cairn Terrier as does

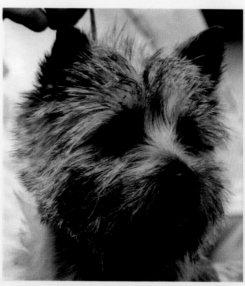

A pretty head study of **Ch. Cairnacre's Scottish Nosegay.** *Owner, Clare Redditt. Photo by Jack DeWitt.*

an eye that is too small. A light eye should be penalized.

One method of determining whether the dog has correct ear and eye placement, both of great importance, is to imagine a line drawn from the tip of the nose to the tip of each ear. Then imagine a line drawn from ear tip to ear tip. The first lines should pass

Ch. Ohioville Rooster breeder-owned by Eleanor Buesing.

directly through the center of each eye, while the line between the ears should be the same length as the two from ear to nose. In other words, a triangle which is practically equal on all three sides should be formed. If these lines are equal in length and the eyes are too much to the outside of the nose to ear lines, they are set too far apart. Conversely, if they fall inside the lines, they are too close together and make the face look pinched. If the line between the ears is quite a bit short, then the ears are set or carried too high on the head giving the look of the Scottish Terrier. If that line is much longer than the nose to ear line, the ears are set too far apart. As far as just the expression itself goes, it does not seem to matter if the skull itself is a bit narrow and the muzzle a tad too long as long as everything falls into place in the nose/eye/ear lines.

Sometimes you will hear breeders talk about cat-faced Cairns. If you look carefully at a cat and draw the same imaginary lines, you will find the same equilateral triangle along with a broad skull and short muzzle. So although a cat and a Cairn look nothing alike, the geometry, so to speak, is similar. Both are structured for strength.

The actual skull of the Cairn is broad between the ears. Also, the zygomatic arch, the bony ridge that forms the lower border of the eye socket and extends back to the rear of the skull below the ear, is easily felt as it stands out and adds width to the skull. The muzzle gradually tapers to somewhat of a point, but not one as sharp as that of the fox. It is full and strong, but not so full as to appear boxy or coarse. The proportions of the skull in both

Ch. Woodmist Grey Heath owned by Susan C. Vertz.

Ch. Feldspar's Bit O'Butterscotch owned by Susan C. Vertz.

width and length are necessary to anchor the muscles that give the jaws their uncommon strength. A muzzle-to-top-skull ratio of four to five gives the proper fulcrum or focal point at the mandibular joint for strength in the bite. A muzzle too long or snipey loses strength, as it is not as well muscled as one that is correct. A muzzle too short might result in small or even missing teeth.

The Cairn's teeth are larger than one would expect. Any dog used for bolting badgers and other animals fully capable of defending themselves to the death must come equipped with teeth equal to the task. Small teeth against a badger or an otter would be similar to a pocket knife against a machete. There should be 20 teeth in the upper jaw, two molars, four pre-molars, and a canine on each side plus six incisors between the canine teeth. On the lower jaw there should be 22 teeth, the extra two being molars. It is not unusual for Cairns to be missing some teeth, most often incisors or pre-molars. However, it is important to breed for the correct mouths, including bite and number of teeth.

The correct bite is either scissors or level. The scissors bite is more commonly found and is preferred. In the scissors bite, the upper incisors just overlap the lower incisors, touching them when the mouth is shut. The lower canines lie snugly between the upper canines and the upper incisors. A level bite has differing definitions in different breeds, but in the Cairn Terrier it means that the cutting surfaces of the upper and lower incisors meet edge to edge rather than the upper incisors overlapping the lower. The position of the canine teeth remains the same. A level bite tends to wear down the incisors more quickly.

A bite is considered overshot when there is too much overlap between the upper and lower incisors. There is no physical contact between the two. Often the lower canines will not mesh properly with the upper ones. This is usually due to a weak or receding lower jaw.

In Cairn Terriers, the upper and lower jaws often seem to grow at different rates. If you have a puppy at 12 weeks who has an overshot mouth but in every other way is a prospect you want to keep, it is recommended that you hold on and wait out the full growth of the jaws. More often than not, the lower jaw will catch up to the upper jaw at six to nine or even ten months of age.

An undershot jaw is a different story. When the bite is undershot, the lower jaw is obviously longer than the upper jaw resulting in the lower incisors overlapping the upper ones. There is no physical contact between lower and upper incisors. A milder form of the undershot mouth is the reverse scissors bite where the lower incisors erupt in front of the upper incisors but there is actual physical contact between the two. Both a reverse scissors bite and an undershot bite are incorrect and should be severely penalized in the show ring. Unlike the puppy with an overshot mouth, a puppy who is undershot at ten to 12 weeks will probably remain that way. Luckily, an undershot mouth is not as common as an overshot one.

The worst problem is the wry mouth. This is when the sides of the jaws grow at different rates. Perhaps the upper right side grows faster

Ch. Cairnkeep Kim-E-Cairn Geordi. Photo by Dawn Burdick.

than any other section and the others never catch up. It is actually possible to have a dog who is both undershot on one side and overshot or level on the other. In this bite, the molars usually will not mesh, causing problems in chewing. This, along with the other faulty bites, should be penalized in the show ring and eliminated from the breeding program.

THE FRONT AND REAR ASSEMBLY

Picture a bicycle in your mind. It has a front wheel, a back wheel, and a frame to which both are attached. Notice that both wheels are the same size as well as being perfectly round. The seat and pedals are affixed at a point where the center of gravity makes them most efficient. All fit together in such a way that the minimum amount of energy required to push the pedals will result in both wheels turning in unison to move the bike forward.

Now picture the same bike with the front wheel larger than the back one. It would take the back wheel more revolutions than the front to cover the same ground. The same would be true if the back wheel were larger than the front. Not only would the bike be out of balance, with you likely to vault over the handlebars, but the front would be spinning like crazy trying to keep up with the push from the rear. If the wheel sprockets were loose, the wheels would wobble. And if the frame of

Ch. Feldspar's Scarlet Doublet owned by Susan C. Vertz. Photo by Patricia Holmes.

the bike were crooked or the wheels not perfectly round, covering ground would be even more of an effort.

Thus it is with the front and rear assembly of the Cairn Terrier. Front and rear legs are attached to a frame, the body skeleton of the dog, by means of muscles and ligaments. If the front and rear do not match or balance each other, such as an over–angulated rear with a straight front, movement will be affected. Loose shoulders result in a wobbly front gait. If the frame is too short, too long, or otherwise incorrect movement is also affected in a negative way.

Angulation is probably the most talked about problem with both

Ch. Brehannon's Mista Rhett, a C.T.C.A. Best in Sweepstakes winner owned by Ken Kauffman.

fronts and rears. It can also be the most confusing to those not familiar with the term. Shoulder layback is another term that is difficult to explain but important to understand. Starting with the front assembly, we will attempt to clarify both terms.

You have probably heard the old children's song which talks about the hip bone being connected to the thigh bone, the thigh bone connected to the knee bone, and so on. Well, angulation is simply the angle at which these bones are connected. The bones we mostly concern ourselves with in the front assembly are usually the scapula, or shoulder blade, and the humerus, or upper arm. We are told that these bones should meet each other at a 90-degree angle. If you are not used to dealing with angles, picturing this can be difficult. A 90-degree angle is what you see when you

look at the door frame and its relation to the floor where the two meet. Now tip that angle over sideways a bit and you have the ideal angulation of the shoulder. Too hard? I agree.

Let's try something simpler. First, we will start with 45 degrees rather than 90 degrees since this seems easier for most people to see in relation to their dog's shoulders. To do this, raise your left hand up in front of you, palm facing away, and hold it there. Now, rotate it so that your thumb is parallel to the ground. If your hand is still relaxed and is pretty normal, the angle formed between your thumb and your index finger is just about 45 degrees (if you spread your thumb as far away from your fingers as possible, you will have a spread of approximately 90 degrees).

Okay, now place your relaxed left hand against the shoulder assembly of your Cairn with the

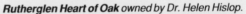

Rutherglen Heart of Oak owned by Dr. Helen Hislop.

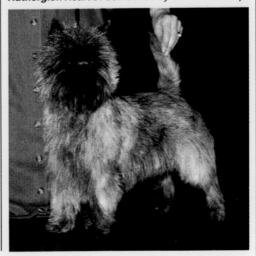

base of your thumb at the point of shoulder where the upper arm and the scapula, or shoulder blade, meet. Keep your thumb parallel to the ground. Your Cairn's scapula should run directly under your index finger up to the tip of his shoulder blade. If it falls more in line with any of your other fingers, such as the middle one, your Cairn has shoulders that are a bit steep or straight. Just feel for the top of the shoulder blades at the base of the neck. Do the tips of the blades match up with your index finger? If they do, you are well on your way to proper shoulder layback and angulation.

Now open your hand so that the fingers are still together but your thumb is as stretched out as far as possible. There you have your approximate 90 degrees. Place your thumb along the upper arm and again, the scapula should fall under your index finger.

Length of upper arm is very important. If the upper arm length does not match the shoulder blade length, movement will be restricted. This is a problem in Cairns and one should breed carefully in order to obtain and

Ch. Chasand's Mighty Avenger. Owner, Glenna Barnes.

BREED
PETRULIS

keep the correct length of upper arm. The best way to tell if they match is to measure them. One quick but not completely accurate way to do this is to simply lift up the front leg on the side you want to measure by bending the knee and putting the foot up toward the elbow. You should be able to clearly see the tip of the shoulder blade and the elbow of the dog. If you drop a straight line from the tip of the shoulder blade, it should run directly into the elbow. If you have a short upper arm, the line will fall behind the elbow instead.

Watching your dog move will let you know how well he reaches forward with his front legs. Sometimes a dog with a somewhat steep scapula but with excellent

length of upper arm will reach out in front of himself almost, and I say almost, as well as a dog with correctly laid back shoulders.

I have mentioned shoulder layback here as part of the terminology used in describing a front assembly. Layback is the term used for the slope of the scapula from the joint with the humerus toward the rear of the dog. Ideally this is the previously mentioned 45-degree angle from a horizontal line drawn through this joint. However, it can also refer to more than just the angulation of the scapula. The shoulders should not only slant at the correct angle to the rear but should also slant slightly inward so that they are closer together at the withers than at the shoulder

Ch. Terriwood's Artful Dresser, a Canadian BIS winner and littermate to American BIS Ch. Terriwood's Best Dressed, both Fancy Dresser sons. Owned by Curt and Joyce Whall.

joint. Shoulders that are slightly inclined this way and have proper musculature holding them to the frame of the dog are called well-knit. Often if the scapula slants back but not inward, the entire front assembly hangs loosely from the body frame and results in loaded (too muscled) or loose shoulders. This affects front movement in any one of several ways, all incorrect, depending on the rest of the front construction.

Bronze statue of Ch. Cairnwood's Quince.

Interestingly, if you have a dog with shoulders laid in too close, he will not be able to lower his head for food or water as the tips of the shoulder blades literally rubbing together will prevent him from doing so. One indicator of this is a dog who always lies down to eat or drink. He is not lazy. He cannot get his head down low enough any other way.

It should be noted that very few breeds actually have the perfect 90-degree angulation. More often seen and still acceptable is a 45-degree layback of the shoulder coupled with a slightly less angulated upper arm. Unacceptable is what is known as a straight shoulder. Here the shoulder layback is much more upright and often has a corresponding poorly angulated upper arm. This is often referred to as a steep front. A steep front or poorly laid back shoulder will

cause the dog's neck to look short. It will often appear as if it has been stuck on the body as an afterthought. A dog with a steep shoulder will not have the lovely arch to his neck that contributes to his typey outline or the smooth flow of neck into topline and his reach forward when moving will be quite limited.

Viewed from the front, the dog's legs should fall straight from his shoulders to the ground. There should be no crookedness to the bones. Feet should be compact with toes tightly together, almost like a cat's foot. They can turn out slightly, but be sure that it is just the foot that turns out and not the entire leg. Feet that are "east-west" are a fault. Pads should be thick and hard, nails short. A good shoulder leading into a straight leg is great, but not if it rests on feet that are splayed, toes pointing to the sides, and nails scraping the ground.

The correct front structure is what gives the Cairn his strength for digging. The slightly turned-out front paws allow him to throw the dirt out behind him as he digs so that he will not bury himself in his own tunnel.

THE BODY

The front and rear assemblies would be rather useless without a strong body between them. The body is usually meant to be the chest area in front and the abdomen area behind it. The chest includes the ribs, sternum, and presternum. You can feel the presternum as the protrusion on the front of the chest. Running your hand down the presternum, you merge into the sternum where the front ribs attach. The ribs, sternum, and presternum protect the heart and lungs.

Ch. Brehannon's On A Rampage owned by Ken Kauffman.

Whetstone Annie Hall owned by Nita Haas.

There should be enough chest between the legs so that they do not appear to both drop out of the bottom of the chest itself. While elbows should be tucked neatly into the rib cage, the legs should be spaced far enough apart that they fall from the shoulder. Puppies can be given some leeway, as their chests are not fully mature. Loose puppy movement will often tighten up as the chest drops and everything comes together.

On an adult dog, the chest should fill your hand with a slight roundness when you cup it in your palm with the point of the presternum at the fleshy base of your thumb near the wrist. Too often today you will feel only a flatness with no depth or fullness in this chest area. Ribs need to be well-sprung, meaning slightly rounded, as they spread out from the spine and curve into a more-or-less heart shape as they taper to the sternum. There needs to be enough spring of rib for heart and lungs to work easily. A shallow chest or flat rib cage will not allow the lungs to fill completely. Of course, the heart must work harder to pump more blood carrying less oxygen to other parts of the body. Imagine your Cairn out hunting, digging into a badger's den, and suddenly running out of steam just as he confronts his quarry. He would hardly have the strength required by the standard to bolt a rabbit, much less a badger.

You do not want a round rib cage, referred to as barrel-shaped, as it would hinder movement, especially when going to ground. Nor do you want a flat rib cage, called slab-sided. Viewed from the front, the ribs should be shaped like an egg standing on its point.

Improper spring of rib and chest can cause problems in gait. A chest with insufficient depth or width often causes crossing over in the front. When the feet are fully extended in a forward

Ch. Sharolaine's For Pete Sake, a son of C.T.C.A. specialty winner Ch. Cairnlea's Robson. Owner, Peggy Beisel McIlwain.

motion, they cross over an imaginary line under the center of the dog. Often one foot will actually cross over in front of the other. This is readily seen as the dog is coming toward you at a trot.

The term topline is usually used when referring to the Cairn's back. By definition, it is actually the outline of the dog from the base of the ears to the base of the tail. However, since most people mean back when they say topline,

Shin Pond Teddy Bear owned by Lyn Serino.

the two are pretty much synonymous. It would be impossible for a Cairn to have a level topline if the actual definition were used.

The Cairn's back should be level. It should not slope downward from withers to tail nor should there be any arch over the loin. There should not be a sagging in the middle. It certainly

should not be higher at the tail set than at the withers. Any of these conditions would indicate problems in basic structure.

Sometimes a puppy will have an imperfect topline. This can be due to parts of the body growing at different rates. Give him some time to grow into himself to see if the back levels itself.

The back should be medium in length. Medium in this case means not as short as that of a West Highland White Terrier and not as long as that of a Sealyham Terrier. The standard calls for body length to be from $14 \frac{1}{4}$ inches to 15 inches from the front of the chest to the back of the hindquarters. This can be rather difficult to measure. An easier way to check for proper back length in proportion to height (which according to the standard should be 10 inches for dogs and $9 \frac{1}{2}$ inches for bitches) is to measure the dog with either your eye or a ruler from floor to withers and from withers to tail set. These measurements should be equal. You will find that a dog standing 10 inches at the withers should measure 10 inches from withers to tail set, provided the tail is set correctly, of course. You will see that adding the extra inches from withers to presternum and tail set to point of rear should give you the additional overall length of body required.

You will find that bitches usually have a slightly longer back than dogs. This is due to a bit more length in the loin area to allow for carrying puppies. However, the back should never be so long as to appear weak or to give the dog an unbalanced appearance.

The tail should be set on at back level continuing off the spine. It does not sit on top of it as does that of the Fox Terrier or the Scottie. For this reason, a tail carried at one or two o'clock on a relaxed dog is fine. When the dog is excited, the tail should stand straight up. There are some who will even allow the tail to tip just slightly forward as long as it is straight. A tail that curves over the back is called a gay tail and is a significant fault. A gay tail is usually caused by an

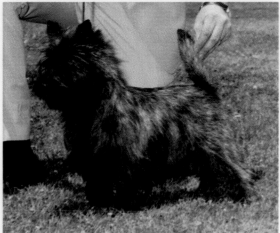

Ch. Cairmar's Boss Man Almin owned by Dr. Helen Hislop.

improper tail set, which can correspondingly be the result of faulty rear construction.

REAR

The rear assembly of the Cairn should match the front in angulation. This gives the dog the required balance for correct movement. Since the rear assembly provides the push, or drive, to propel the dog forward, it is necessary that it is correctly put together. In a dog with correct rear angulation and movement, you can actually see the legs push the body forward. The hocks flex, the feet dig into the ground, and the leg extends out behind the dog in a strong follow-through motion.

A rear can be over- or under-angulated. An over-angulated rear causes several different problems, one or all of which can show up in the same dog. The two faults most often seen are a roach in the back and a faulty gait called crabbing

AmCan. Ch. Terriwood's Best Dressed, a Fancy Dresser son who went Best in Show in 1991, owner-handled by Tom and Karin Godwin.

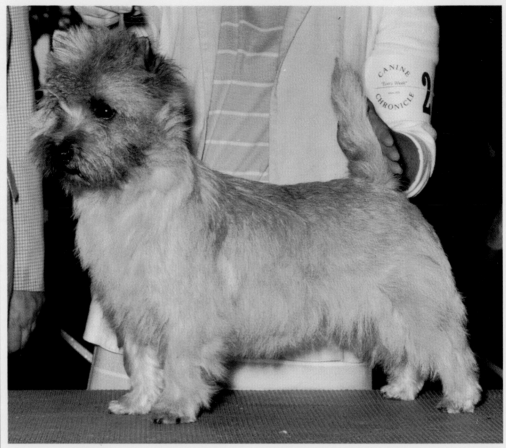

Ch. Foxairn Little Miss Marker, *dam of Ch. Foxairn Tinman. Owners, Sanderson and Margaret McIlwaine. Photo by Martin Booth.*

or sidewinding. This is when the back feet reach so far underneath the dog when they move forward that both front and back feet need to occupy the same space underneath the dog at the same time. In order to compensate, the rear feet come down to one side instead of under the dog. When the dog is moving toward or away from you, you can see all four legs clearly. One hind leg will appear to be between the front legs and the other will be to the outside. The entire spinal column appears to point at an angle instead of straight ahead.

Another compensation is a weaving motion in the rear, seemingly a delaying tactic for the front feet to move out of the way of the rear feet. More often than not, a puppy who moves this way will continue to do so even as an adult. But since puppies can surprise you, it is best to wait a few months before making any firm decisions.

The bones we must look at when we talk angulation in the rear are the pelvis, the upper thighbone or femur, and the second thighbones consisting of the fibula and tibia. Also important is the hock.

The pelvis slopes down from the spine at the base of the tail at a 30-degree angle. It is equipped with a socket, or a ball joint, at the lower end into which the top of the femur fits. The femur angles forward from this joint under and just behind the set of the tail to the stifle joint. This is exactly the reverse of the front angulation where the two shoulder bones, the scapula and the humerus slope toward the rear. The two angles form "parentheses" with the body in between. The angulation in between the pelvis and the femur should match the front. You got it—90 degrees. The second thighs angle back to the hock, which falls straight to the ground. The angulation between the femur and the second thigh (the angle on the back side of the leg just below the "parentheses") is about 110 degrees. A 90-degree angle here would be too severe. A rear that is too over-angulated will cause a sloping topline with the rump lower than

Ch. Goosedown's Tailor Made at nine months of age. Owner's, Pat Hassey and Lynn Hickey.

the withers. This gives the dog a crouching appearance when standing still.

A dog is called straight-stifled when these angles are too wide. The femur, or upper thigh, appears to drop down more than sloping inward. This throws off the angulation of the second thighs and can even cause the hocks to angle instead of standing perpendicular to the ground.

Ch. Fashion Tag of Wildwood, a Ch. Whetstone Halston daughter.

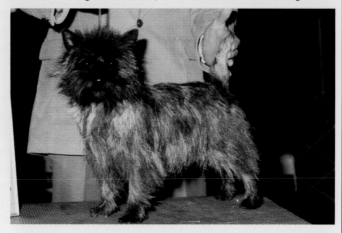

Straight stifles cause a choppy gait with no drive and it takes more steps to cover ground, which in turn takes more energy.

Remember the bicycle with the small back tire spinning madly to keep up with the front tire of normal size? This is similar to straight stifles. Of course, if the front is also straight, the two assemblies are balanced, which is fine, except for the minor problem combined with strong musculature and flexibility provides the push needed in correct movement. Rear pasterns that are too long give the leg the appearance of high hocks. Much energy is wasted by this construction which gives a peculiar pumping motion to the rear. Sometimes it looks almost as if the hock joints are popping when the dog gaits.

Ch. CairnBrae's Hint of Gold owned by Ann F. Kerr.

that both of them are incorrect.

A dog with correct rear angulation will have a wide, well-muscled thigh with a pleasing curve to it. This is a well-bent stifle. This meets the hock joint from which the rear pastern, or metatarsus, drops to the foot. The hocks in the Cairn Terrier should be well let down. This simply means that the rear pastern is not too long and the hock joint is set fairly close to the ground. This

Cow hocks are a major fault as are bowed hocks. Both of these conditions occur when the hock turns in or out from an imaginary line from the hip to the foot. Cow hocks result in restricted movement and closeness in the rear. Sometimes the hocks almost brush against each other. Bowed hocks look like the proverbial cowboy who has ridden his horse for too many years. This causes a waddling movement, which is unsound, not to mention unattractive. Another common fault is the sickle hock. The rear pastern angles slightly forward from hock joint to foot, giving the appearance of a sickle. This fault

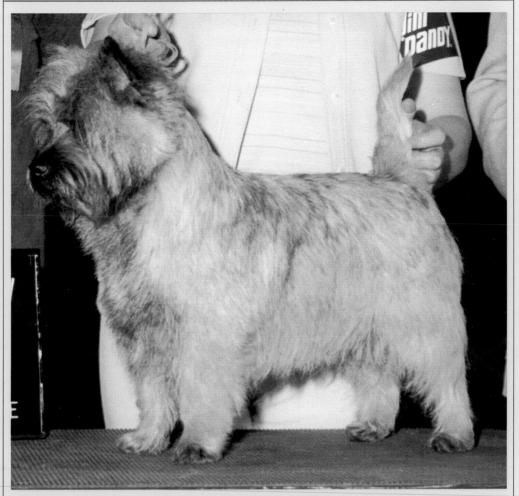

Ch. Cairmar Call To Arms, *a Best in Show Cairn bred, owned, and handled by Betty Marcum.*

also causes restricted movement and is often found in conjunction with straight stifles.

The rear feet should be similar to the front feet except that they are smaller since they are not used for digging. They should turn neither in nor out and should have thick pads and short nails.

When you run your hands over your Cairn, there should be no lumps or bumps obstructing the smooth flow of his neck into his shoulders on to his body and rear assembly. His coat should be hard and profuse. His paw pads should be somewhat calloused in order to handle rough terrain. Feet should be tight without splayed toes. There should be no fat. Imagine a jolt of electricity just waiting to go into action and you have a Cairn Terrier.

A puppy grows up...

The future **Ch. Bramblewood's Stetson:** *(above left)* at two weeks of age; *(above right)* at five weeks of age; *(below)* at 12 weeks of age.

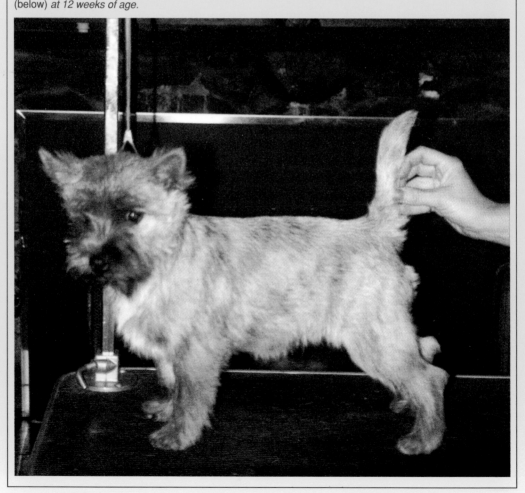

Ch. Bramblewood's Stetson: (above) *at five months of age;* (below) *at 14 months of age. Photographed by Joe Rinehart.*

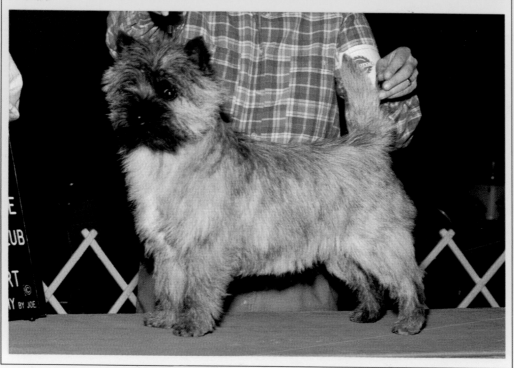

A lovely female puppy at six weeks of age. Photo by Janis Whitcomb.

Selecting Your Cairn

by Chris Walkowicz

PICKING THE RIGHT PUP

Buying a puppy should not be an impulsive endeavor; it is never wise to rush out and buy just any puppy that catches your shopping eye. The more time and thought you invest, the greater your satisfaction with your new companion. And if this new companion is to be purely a pet, its background and early care will affect its future health and good temperament. It is always essential that you choose a properly raised puppy from healthy, well-bred stock.

You must seek out an active, sturdy puppy with bright eyes and an intelligent expression. If the puppy is friendly, that's a major plus, but you don't want one that is hyperactive nor do you want one that is dull and listless. The coat should be clean and plush, with no signs of fleas or other parasites. The premises should be clean, by sight and smell, and the proprietors should be helpful and knowledgeable. A reputable seller wants his customers satisfied and will therefore represent the puppy fairly. Let good common sense guide your purchase, and choose a *reliable*, well-recommended source that you know has well-satisfied customers. Don't look for a bargain, since you may end up paying many times over in future veterinarian bills, not to mention disappointment and heartache if your pet turns out not to be well.

SELECTING A PUPPY TO SHOW

A puppy might grow up to be a good pet. Or he can be much more than that: a blue-ribbon winner, a helpmate, a marvel of ability and, certainly, a beloved companion. The pup's future possibilities are restricted only by the owner's goals for him and enhanced by knowledgeable selection of this future Super Dog.

Choosing to share our lives with a dog is only the first step of a decision-filled time. We must determine also which breed best suits us and our lifestyle. It's wise to be prepared for several questions that will arise: Male or female? Adult or puppy? Did we select this breed for its special qualities and abilities or simply because we like its appearance or temperament?

Within a breed—even within a litter—personality differences are found, and buyers should specify whether they want the one who bounces off the walls or the one who sleeps 23 hours a day. Other preferences, such as size or color, might be stated. A potential exhibitor should say whether competition in obedience or achieving a championship is a priority.

MAKING CONNECTIONS

When a serious fancier chooses a dog to fulfill hopes and dreams, more is involved than simply finding a litter of the chosen breed and picking the pup with the waggiest tail or the lickingest tongue. First, a breeder with an impeccable reputation must be found. For those who are already involved in the dog world, it's less difficult to make connections because they are aware of preferences in structure or in ability and have an idea as to which lines produce well in these respects.

The recent enthusiast may have to overcome a few more obstacles, but the goal is worth the trouble. When people want the best, they haunt the places where the best are found. When Cape Cod tourists crave a fresh clam bake, they go to the beach, not the all-night grocery. The finest wines are found at first-class restaurants, not at a lunch counter. And the same is true of dogs. According to various interests, the superior dogs will be at shows, trials or tests.

While studying the dogs who are esthetically pleasing and who perform in the manner admired, make notes on the kennels that boast the winners. Which sires and dams produce consistently?

Bramblewood's Silver Lining at five weeks of age. At this age puppies are very curious. Note the dark points on the tail tip and toes.

Five-day-old puppies photographed by Dawn Burdick.

Their owners are the blue-ribbon breeders. Even if these kennels do not have puppies available, they are the places to start. Most owners are willing and able to recommend other breeders, and these people usually refer you only to places that they would buy from themselves. Giving a poor reference reflects on their own reputation; therefore, they stick to those with a four-star rating.

Starting at the root with a quality breeder allows a buyer to branch off if necessary. Show kennels have a monetary as well as an emotional investment at stake and seek excellence in the handlers, groomers and veterinarians with whom they do business. These professionals are additional sources of referrals. They often know who has litters, as well as who has top-notch animals and a squeaky clean reputation. Handlers, vets and groomers have a stake in the matter, too, because they might gain a client from someone who follows their lead and is pleased.

Dog clubs can supply reliable contacts as well. Many have a breeder index or answering services for just this purpose. The American Kennel Club can furnish the secretaries' names of sanctioned all-breed and specialty clubs, both locally and nationally. Often clubs are listed with the Chamber of Commerce or in the telephone book. The Kennel Club of Great Britain is the appropriate

Seek out an active, sturdy puppy with bright eyes and an intelligent expression. Owner, Suzette M. Heider.

interest.

Published breed books, such as this one, display photos of top-winning dogs and descriptions of the kennels that produced them. The motto, "Records live, opinions die" is a truism. Any kennel that claims winners numbering in the double digits or above has begun its own records.

Of course, the professional breeder who is just starting up the ladder offers advantages as well. Because he doesn't have the widespread reputation, he is less likely to have waiting lists. Frequently, the person from whom he bought his bitch or who owns the stud he used will refer inquiries to him.

Although cost should not be number one on our list when searching for a companion, it is a consideration for most of us, and a beginner seldom can demand the prices of the established breeder. If the dedicated newcomer has bought his foundation stock from a reputable kennel, very likely he will have animals for sale that are comparable in quality to his mentor's. Not everyone who looks for a new, snazzy car can afford to buy a Mercedes. Some of us have to be satisfied with a well-built Chevrolet. And that Chevy can be attractive and dependable too. We don't always have to buy top-of-the-line to obtain quality, as long as we stay away from the junkyard.

source for British residents, as is the Canadian Kennel Club.

Some clubs have a code of ethics which the breeders must sign and adhere to in order to be recommended. Money-minded profiteers are seldom found within the ranks of clubs because they have no interest in supporting and working at shows, seminars or canine charity fundraisers.

Ads in canine magazines and newspapers are costly, and kennels who advertise are usually secure, well-established businesses with owners who have a reputation to maintain. It is up to us to determine just how fine that reputation is. "Brag" ads trumpeting the kennel's latest Field Trial Champion or Best in Show Winner can give clues of success within a specific field of

NETWORKING

In conducting any type of research, one lead suggests another. A contact list mushrooms and grows, giving the buyer several options.

When contacting a well-known kennel and finding no puppies available, it is helpful to ask, "Can you recommend someone?" Or, "I just love your stud, Alf (or your bitch, Tigger). Does anyone have puppies with those lines?" Who can resist a compliment like that?

Ask breeders whether they belong to a local club and the national breed club. Club membership shows a sustained interest in the breed and in dogs.

SEARCHING FOR SUPER DOG

Finding the ideal dog is not a whit easier than looking for the ideal mate. Of course, it's a bit less complicated to rid ourselves of an unwanted beast if it's the four-legged kind, but failure is not the object of conducting this search. It's finding a buddy, a companion, one who appeals to us in every sense and will still do so when he's old, gray and pot-bellied.

When it comes to welcoming a new member into a family, spending the time to find the right addition is well worth the effort. It can't be done by placing an ad in the personal want ad section: Tall, athletic man of 40 desires a jogging companion who is cute, fuzzy and has floppy ears.

How then? Buyers should look at several examples of the breed before plunging into a ten-to-fifteen-year commitment. Many who have experience and have developed an "eye" know immediately whether or not a particular litter is going to offer promise. But those who are buying a dog for the first time or who are engaged in an initial search for this particular breed need to see more than one specimen to make such a decision. And it's best not to base a choice on a picture in a book or a television commercial, unless you've had the opportunity to see

Seven- and eight-week-old puppies sired by Ch. Cairmar Boss Man Almin.

the dog in reality and in action.

Certain questions arise that can only be answered through a one-on-one session. Can I live with the energy of this breed/individual? Is this dog too aloof for me?

Even if the dog of our dreams lives 2,000 miles away and it's impossible to make a speculative jaunt, buyers can observe the breed at shows or by hunting down a specimen that lives within 200 miles. Two hundred miles is

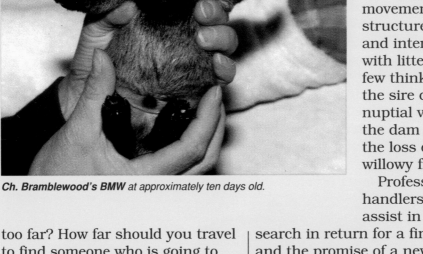

Ch. Bramblewood's BMW at approximately ten days old.

too far? How far should you travel to find someone who is going to inhabit a corner of your life, your home and your heart for the next dozen years?

When the selection is narrowed down to one or two breeders and litters, and it comes to making a choice of the individual, this can be done even if the 2,000-mile

trek isn't feasible. Of course, we have already ascertained that the breeder is reputable, so relying on his expertise and experience with the lines is helpful. Matchmaking is his business. He has everything to gain by ensuring the happiness of the new owner (and thereby the pup's) and everything to lose if it turns out to be a match made in hell.

Photos are a necessity in making a long-distance selection. Some modern-technology breeders offer videos to prospective buyers, demonstrating each puppy's movement, structure, attitude and interaction with littermates. A few think to film the sire during the nuptial visit and the dam prior to the loss of her willowy figure.

Professional handlers can assist in the search in return for a finder's fee and the promise of a new client. If the pro appears at the door with a scraggly hag instead of the voluptuous vamp of our dreams, it's no go and no dough.

ONE ON ONE

If we're fortunate enough to live in the same vicinity as the kennel, we can conduct our own evaluation and perhaps participate in a temperament or aptitude test of the litter. Certain other subtleties can be assessed as well, such as the breeder's rapport with his dogs. An unspoken but obvious bond should be present, passing from one to the other. . . a look of devotion when the dam looks at her owner. . . pride shining on the face of the breeder and soft affection for the dogs in his eyes. . . an almost automatic caress of a velvet ear during the buyer's interview. . . a wet nose nuzzling under an arm.

Happy, healthy dogs greet visitors at the door. Firm but gentle corrections are given and obeyed—at least partially, during the excitement of having guests. Needless to say, the sire and dam must be sound in mind and body as well as typical of the breed— that is, they look like Beagles instead of Bassets or vice versa. Although the sire is seldom a roommate of the dam, the breeder should have photos and a pedigree of the dog available for viewing.

Buyers should be prepared to ask questions as well as to answer them. Does the breeder belong to a club, has he ever shown, and do any of his dogs have titles? Does he linebreed, inbreed or outcross? Negative answers do not necessarily mean "Buyer Beware." The breeder should have answers,

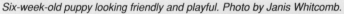

Six-week-old puppy looking friendly and playful. Photo by Janis Whitcomb.

Six-week-old litter photographed by Janis Whitcomb.

however, to educated questions and not say, "Huh?" or "Got no time for such foolishness."

It is our duty to discover whether any problems exist in our breed and whether the breeder has taken steps to avoid them. For instance, are his breeding animals OFA1 certified for good hips and CERF1 cleared for normal eyes? VWD1, OCD1, hypothyroidism, deafness and epilepsy, in addition to other conditions, are hereditary and should not be present in breeding stock. If we're interested in becoming breeders ourselves, a free-whelping line and superlative foundation stock are pluses.

When appropriate, ask about and examine for entropion, earsets, incorrect bites and missing teeth, as well as other problems that may be known to appear in the breed. If we've done our homework, mismarks and improper coats should be apparent, but one should be aware of less obvious breed faults also.

MAKING THE GRADE

Those who wish to conduct formal temperament tests should do so when the puppies are seven weeks of age. These tests not only help breeders and buyers determine which pups are over-aggressive or horribly shy (hopefully none), but they show the range of good temperaments and obedience aptitude.

Pups should be tested separately, preferably on new turf by someone unknown to them. When the tester or surroundings is familiar, tendencies may be hidden or exaggerated.

In each instance, note whether the pups are bold, shy or curious.

If a pup startles or is hesitant, does he recover and respond to the tester positively?

Social tests:

1. Observe the pup's reaction to the strange place and to a stranger. Is he bold, shy or curious? Note whether he bounces around immediately confident, hides in a corner or takes a moment to gain his composure and then begins to explore.

2. The tester should bend or kneel and call the puppy to him in a friendly manner, clapping or whistling if he wishes.

3. The tester stands and walks away, calling to the pup.

Dominance tests:

4. Rolling the pup on his back, the tester holds him in place for 30 seconds.

5. A stranger pets the pup on his head and looks directly at him, putting his face close to the pup's.

6. Pick up the pup with hands under the belly; hold elevated for 30 seconds.

Alertness/obedience tests:

7. Crumple noisy paper or rattle a stone inside a can.

8. Toss the paper or a toy to see if the pup retrieves and returns the object.

9. Drag a towel or similar object in front of the pup. Does he show

Over chip, over dale, we will hit the dusty trail, as the Cairns go rolling along... Owner, Pauli Christy.

curiosity and follow?

Responses:

The bold, naughty or aggressive pup reacts immediately, sometimes barking or biting. This pup struggles during the restraint or dominance tests. He might grab at the tester's clothing. A top dog such as this one needs a dominant owner, a person who is willing—and able—to train, discipline and maintain control.

At the other end of the scale is the pup who shrinks away, shows disinterest or hides. He might cry or give in immediately during the restraint and dominance tests. The underdog takes a patient owner, one who is willing to encourage and socialize.

In between is the pup who is friendly, accepting and rather middle of the road. He might be hesitant, but is cooperative in most efforts. This one should fit in almost any home!

The ideal obedience prospect would willingly follow and come. He'd also be alert and show curiosity; he'd run after the toy, pick it up and return it to the tester.

When searching for the perfect Cairn pup, find a breeder who is a step above the rest. Photo by Dawn Burdick.

NARROWING IT DOWN

Breeders have the additional advantage of living with the litter for eight or more weeks. They are the best ones to know which pup is the pack leader, which one follows docilely and which one tries to topple the king of the mountain off his perch. Notes should be made on eager or picky eaters. Individual descriptions using such adjectives as rowdy or laid-back, outgoing or aloof, and independent or willing to please are helpful during matchmaking.

When initial contact is made with the seller, we should specify what type of personality is desired in our future pet. A "type A" perfectionist or workaholic will find it difficult to live

Before choosing your puppy, observe the entire litter interacting with one another. This is **Ch. Goosedown's Tailor Made** as a puppy with his littermates.

with a rough-and-tumble, devil-take-care livewire who is trying out for the next *Rambo* sequel. Nor would the 78-year-old gent who likes to snooze by the evening fire want to go home with the canine yo-yo. (But this pup would be perfect for the athletic man wanting a jogging companion in that personal ad.)

The one absolute no-no is picking a dog because you feel sorry for him. Sorry lasts a long time. Rarely does a new home cure timidity, illness or anti-social behavior.

An owner who intends to field trial or hunt with his dog wants to find one who has a good nose and high energy. Dangle a bird feather on a rod and see whether the pup reacts by flash or sight pointing.

Marked timidity shown during household pan rattling or door slamming wouldn't fare well for a dog who's expected to join in the hunt. A bold, independent dog who shows curiosity is desirable.

SELECTING THE FLYER

Those of us who have visions of red, white and blue Best in Show rosettes dancing in our heads look at type, structure, movement, and a certain indefinable quality called presence. The best way to do this is to view the pups two or three at a time, ideally in a place which allows free movement and play: a fenced yard or a large room.

Any pup who exhibits disqualifying or serious faults should be eliminated from choice and from the examination site

*This cool Cairn is **The Red Knight of Misty Moor CDX, Can. CD.** Photo by Dawn Burdick.*

immediately. We can't take the chance of a sweet face turning us from our goal. Dogs of every breed who are blind or deaf, display viciousness or cryptorchidism (undescended testicles) as well as those that are neutered are specifically disqualified from conformation competition. Most breeds have additional disqualifications or serious faults—for example, size, color, coat or bite—and potential show buyers must be aware of these.

While the puppies are playing, look for the strut of canine royalty. Some dogs are born to show and they know it. They exhibit the panache of Clark Gable as Rhett Butler or sparkle like opening night at the opera. Given the choice, the ring-wise will opt for the pup with a less elegant neck and more charisma than for a deadhead swan.

Buyers should use the breed standard as a blueprint and study the pups, using heads and eyes rather than hearts. First on the list is a "typey" litter, followed by the pup that is most representative. Pretend Great Aunt Minnie has seen only a picture of this breed. Which one could she look at and say, "Ah ha, *this* is a ...." Ideally, this pup will also possess the other physical requirements and have the spirit that makes him or her a special dog.

While examining bone, topline, shoulder and rear angulation, breadth and depth of chest, and length of body, a person should compare this to the blueprint standard in mind. Feel coat quality, taking into consideration the puppy coat. Is it fine or dense as required? Harsh or silky? The color, of course, should be acceptable. There is no sense in battling upstream with such an obvious fault which is so easily eliminated from selection.

Although personalities differ in dogs, sometimes with a wide normal range, temperament should be typical of the breed. No one buys a Chihuahua to guard their property, and probably few expect a Mastiff to curl up in their laps beyond infancy. The pup who displays confidence is always a better choice than one who cringes and shrinks from human touch.

Even if the standard calls for aloofness, puppies are usually blessed with an innocent sweetness. This characteristic makes them a delight to their family even if they grow to adulthood and snub everyone else. Whether the affection is demonstrated by a glow in the eyes, a single thump of the tail or bounding ecstasy at our approach, our dogs should like us . . . even if they don't like anyone else on earth.

Puppies *bounce,* puppies *boinnng,* puppies *galumph.* But, given enough time, the one who is put together in the proper way will demonstrate a baby version of

These boots are made for walking...and a couple of Cairn pups. Owner, Pauli Christy.

exciting adult movement. We must be prepared to catch a glimpse into the future.

BUYING A PIECE OF THE FUTURE

Some buyers place a deposit for a puppy sight unseen, sometimes even before the litter is born or bred! When we find a breeder who is producing the style, type and movement we want, it might be necessary to make a reservation long before our future dream pup sets paw on the ground. After all, if we admire what is trotting out of this kennel's gates, we should realize a few others might have recognized its quality as well. Breeders who consistently produce well often have long waiting lists.

Before selecting a kennel to honor with the purchase, other factors can be discussed with the seller in advance. Be aware of the guarantee offered, what the contract covers and whether this kennel has established a reputation for standing behind its dogs.

Certain minimal records should accompany every pup: a pedigree, a registration blank, medical records, feeding and grooming instructions, a sales contract and some type of guarantee.

Registration papers are a necessity for the serious fancier who wishes to show and breed. ILP (Individual Listing Privilege) may be shown in obedience as can Limited Registration dogs who may also participate in a few instinct tests. They may not, however, be exhibited in the conformation ring. The American Kennel Club requires ILP dogs (other than those in the Miscellaneous Classes) to be spayed or neutered, and the Limited Registration stamp, begun in 1990, prevents the limited dog's progeny from being

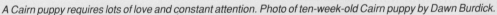

A Cairn puppy requires lots of love and constant attention. Photo of ten-week-old Cairn puppy by Dawn Burdick.

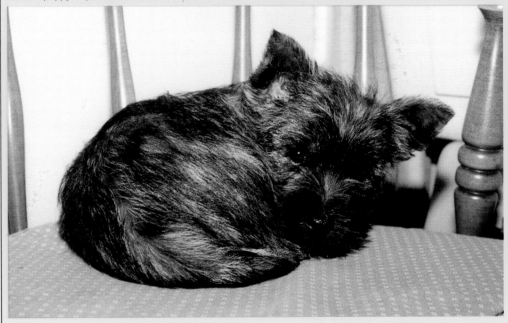

registered. These steps were taken by the AKC to discourage indiscriminate breeding practices.

A pedigree should contain at least three generations, with four to six being preferable. Pedigrees tell us more than the names and titles of ancestors. The knowledgeable can see whether a pup is linebred, outcrossed or inbred, and health certifications such as OFA and CERF numbers are often included, as are colors. A pedigree strong in obedience titles should give an indication that the pup's family demonstrates trainability and intelligence. Likewise, several championship titles are encouraging. Quality begets quality.

The best time to pick your Cairn puppy is between the ages of eight to ten weeks. By this time puppies have already learned canine socialization skills from their dam and littermates. Owner, Phil Shoop.

An eight-week-old pup should not have a lengthy medical record, but this paper should note a physical exam and at least one combination inoculation. If the litter has been wormed, this should also be noted.

A good age to pick a puppy is when the litter is from eight to ten weeks old. By this time, they have learned canine socialization skills from their dam and littermates. With plenty of TLC given by the breeder as a background, sound puppies easily transfer their affection to a new family.

Lines and breeds vary, but many knowledgeable breeders prefer to pick their show prospects between eight to twelve weeks of age. Follow the breeder's advice; nobody knows the lines better than he does.

Occasionally the subject of co-ownership arises. This may create the best of times or the worst of times; it certainly forges the members of a paper relationship into the best of friends or festers them into the worst of enemies. An offer of co-ownership does signify that the breeder has faith in the dog. After all, he wouldn't want to co-own a poor specimen.

A decision can be made depending upon the strings of the co-ownership and whether the two parties can work together. Simple co-ownership agreements may require one puppy back from a breeding or stud rights. More complicated contracts demand half a litter—or half of every litter, exhibition requirements, hiring an expensive professional handler, or more. If breeder and buyer are congenial and willing to bend when situations not covered in the contract arise, a co-ownership can be an opportunity to purchase a dog or bitch normally beyond our price range.

Puppies come ready to use—all wound up and ready for action. This is **Kirkshire's Smuggler** *photographed by Pat Holmes.*

PAPER WORK

Sales contracts should cover the information listed on the registration blank, along with various requirements.

Guarantees usually cover a short period of time until the buyer can take the puppy to a veterinarian. If there is a problem at that time, a full refund should be given. Most reputable buyers also give a health guarantee covering various congenital defects which arise by the age of one year—one year, because most have appeared by that time; congenital, because the seller cannot be expected to cover injuries or illnesses. Should a congenital defect appear after this age (such as failure to OFA certify at two years of age), the seller should still be willing to discuss a replacement.

Sellers' show puppy contracts usually cover serious and disqualifying faults as stipulated in the breed standard. All contracts and guarantees should be read carefully by the buyer. If any clauses are objectionable or questionable, ask for an explanation before signing.

Although the pup won't come with an operator's manual that directs you to "Put tab A into slot A" or have a bag attached with extra nuts and bolts, instructions should be part of the package. This will cover suggested puppy food, feeding schedule, housebreaking suggestions, and grooming particulars. Written advice on crates, training classes, and recommended reading material may have more than one use. It helps fill the wee morning hours when the pup misses his warm, fuzzy siblings and wails his loss to the world.

Sales Contract

WHEREAS, _____ , hereinafter called "Seller(s)," is the owner of a _____ show/showable _____ (breed) bitch/dog, further described as:

Registered Name of Dog _____ Call name of Dog _____
Color/Variety _____
Date of Birth _____ Place of Birth _____
Litter/AKC/Foreign Reg. No. _____
Name/Reg. No. of Sire _____
Name/Reg. No. of Dam _____

WHEREAS _____ , hereinafter called "Buyer(s)," is desirous of purchasing the animal described above: NOW, THEREFORE, in consideration of the sum of _____ , payable _____ , the Seller hereby conveys one _____ (quality & breed) bitch/dog to Buyer(s) under the following warranties and conditions and no other warranties or conditions either expressed or implied.

1. That the above described animal is a purebred dog registerable with _____ (Kennel Club) within 180 days following the date of purchase and that a registration application has been given to Buyer(s) as of the date of purchase.

2. That the above-described animal may for any reason be returned to Seller(s) within five days of the time of purchase, and Seller will refund to Buyer(s) the full amount of the purchase price. Buyer(s) shall assume full responsibility for the health, anatomical make-up, appearance and temperament of the above-described animal following said five-day period.

3. In the event severe or disqualifying faults as listed and defined in the attached Breed Standard, and/or crippling congenital faults are found to be present in the above-described animal, on or before one year of age, the Seller(s) agrees to replace said animal with one of equal quality. In the instance Seller(s) is no longer in the business of breeding dogs, 50% of the purchase price shall be refunded.

4. In the event the Buyer(s) feels he must dispose of or sell the above-described animal for any reason, Buyer(s) will notify Seller(s) for first option.

5. That this contract is null and void except for dog of above registered name.

6. Further, _____
_____

7. This writing constitutes the full agreement of the parties.

WHEREFORE, the above-named Seller(s) and Buyer(s) have executed the foregoing contract of sale at _____ a.m./p.m. on this _____ day of _____ , 19 _____.

Buyer _____ Seller _____
Address _____ Address _____
Phone _____ Phone _____

A sample sales contract. Sales contracts should cover the information listed on the registration blank, a long with various requirements.

The purchase is only the beginning of a long relationship between buyer and seller. There are questions to be answered, pleasant stories to be shared and fears to be calmed. Photos of the little guy opening his Christmas presents, bathtime, the teenage uglies, entering his first puppy match and finishing his championship are treasured keepsakes for the breeder.

Sounds complicated, but puppies have an advantage over most purchases with moving parts. They come ready to use, all wound up and ready for action—no batteries needed. Nor is it necessary to plug in the pup to make him wag his tail or wash your face. In case of power failure, we don't even miss the electric blanket.

BENEFITS OF OWNERSHIP

The benefits of owning a pet are many, among them pride, socialization, education, acceptance, responsibility. We are often proud of owning a beautiful animal (remembering that beauty is in the eye of the beholder) whose coat shines with health and whose eyes sparkle with glee at our approach. We can make friends and establish relationships through our dog. Kids and adults both learn responsibility through caring for the pet. We educate ourselves to provide physical care and, if we so desire, the intricacies of the dog world—as far as we want to go. Our dog doesn't care at what stage we stop learning. Acceptance comes because our dog always greets us with affection, no matter what our age, race, creed, size or abilities.

But probably the most important benefit is psychological. No matter what happens in our day-to-day life, there is always someone who cares, someone who asks little in return. Our dog provides us with a reason to rise in the morning, a reason to exercise, a reason to prepare food and, in some cases, a reason to live. We're never alone when we're in the company of a good friend.

Color is one consideration when choosing your Cairn puppy. This is a typical wheaten pup.

Wee Geordie Bit O'Divil at 11 weeks of age. Photo by Janis Whitcomb.

Living with a Cairn

While he is a delight to live with, the Cairn Terrier is not for everyone. Do not forget that this is a big dog in a small body. If you think that a Cocker Spaniel's temperament is ideal, it is most likely that the Cairn Terrier is not for you. However, if you like a little dog with a mind of his own, who will challenge you to meet

You should provide your new Cairn puppy with plenty of toys and a comfortable bed. Owner, Pauli Christy.

him on his own terms, the Cairn could be a match.

PUPPY BASICS

If you buy a Cairn Terrier puppy, chances are you will be bringing him or her home at around nine to 12 weeks of age. As with any puppy, be sure to be prepared with food that the

breeder has recommended, toys, and a crate or kennel that will be his own private room. Puppies need breaks from us just as much as we need time to ourselves. A kennel, such as an airline crate, is your puppy's safe harbor. A puppy obtained from a good breeder will already be crate-trained and will go to his "bedroom" when he is tired. Contrary to uninformed people's opinions that crates are cruel, dogs are den-dwelling animals and a crate is a natural cave-like den to them. Do not disturb your puppy when he has gone there on his own. It is his way of saying "time out."

HOUSETRAINING

Cairns are usually quite easy to housetrain, especially if they are at least 12 weeks old when they come home. By that age, they are physically able to contain themselves as long as they are let out frequently. The breeder will often have them paper trained already. They are naturally clean dogs and will use papers if they are provided.

The easiest way to housetrain a

Wee Geordie Bit O'Divil at four months of age. Photo by Janis Whitcomb.

Cairn is to keep him within eyesight at all times so accidents cannot happen. Take him out after every nap, no matter how short, and after every meal. A rough and tumble play session will stimulate him as well, so take him out after a few minutes of play.

You can tell when your puppy needs to defecate, as he will sniff the ground and circle. If he does this in the house, this is your signal to take him outside immediately. Always say something like "let's go outside" and then always take him to the same area of the yard. Praise him profusely when he has accomplished his task. The puppy who never has a chance to urinate or defecate in the house will soon realize that outside is the place to go. The only time to punish him for relieving himself inside is when he is actually caught in the act. A firm "NO" is all the punishment he will need. Then take him outside to finish his business and praise him if he does. If you find an "accident" in the house, it only means that you have not done your job of supervising him to prevent the problem.

Some Cairns will urinate when they first see you or when you bend over to pick them up. This is called submissive urination and most puppies will outgrow it.

When you cannot be with your puppy, be sure he is in an enclosed area with papers, his crate, and some toys. If you are going out for just a couple of hours, you can put him in his crate where he will probably sleep. Puppies will rarely soil their crates, as it would be like soiling their own bedrooms. Never leave a puppy running loose and unsupervised in the house, the yard, or anywhere else where he could get into trouble. After all, even the best puppies have accidents.

OBEDIENCE

The Cairn is affectionate and playful but can be stubborn and willful at times. It seems that his reply to any command is "make me." While this is endearing as he looks at you with that sparkle in his eye, it can be at the very least bothersome when you want him to do something and at the most life-threatening when he darts

Ch. Kirkshire's Spice O'Life becoming familiar with his new surroundings. Owner, Pat Holmes.

into a busy street despite your commands to come. Needless to say, a Cairn should never be let off-lead when not in his own fenced yard.

Cairns need to know that you are the boss. It is far too easy for a Cairn to take over the entire household if given free reign. These little dogs have strong personalities and will do their best to get away with murder. Harsh punishment is not necessary. Usually a firm word or two will suffice as long as you start young and stay consistent. Once a puppy knows you will let him get away with something he should not be doing, he will be sure to repeat it as often as possible.

While obedience training can be trying to your patience, it can be even more trying on your Cairn's. Just remember that your Cairn is smarter than many other breeds. Because of this, he will not "sit" 20 times in a row if you ask him

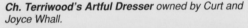

Ch. Terriwood's Artful Dresser owned by Curt and Joyce Whall.

to. He will quickly reason that this is completely boring and will find something else to do. He might decide to comply with your command and sit with his head hung to the ground as if he has been beaten. He could walk over to the opposite end of the room and sit, staring out the window. Or he might just ignore you. Therefore, you must make any training session short and interesting. Use lots of praise and even a treat or two. If you go to an obedience instructor, it would be best to find someone who has worked successfully with short-legged terriers and who understands their inquisitive and demanding intelligence.

DIGGING

Your Cairn will keep you entertained for hours with his games and tricks. These guys are almost cat-like in agility and inventiveness. They will play ball for hours, followed by a game of chase and then still find the energy to dig a hole in your new garden.

Ah yes, the digging instinct is as strong in Cairns today as it was when they were originally bred to go to ground after vermin. If you must have a beautiful lawn and bountiful flower gardens, it would be best to either confine your Cairn to his own special yard or perhaps decide on a dog who does not love to dig as much as you love to garden. Cairns enjoy fresh vegetables and fruits, so you could find your vegetable garden

harvested, especially the carrots, before you are ready. You might even find a tunnel several feet deep with a Cairn hidden inside, if he has an afternoon and a whole yard to himself.

TERRIER TRIALS–USEFUL DIGGING

This digging instinct can be put to good use by actually training your dog to go to ground. He can even earn a title called a Certificate of Gameness, which is

Obedience work with a Cairn is challenging, but rewarding. Owner, Cindy Eli.

only awarded to terriers and a few other breeds who also go to ground. This certificate shows that your Cairn still possesses the hunting and digging instinct of his ancestors. While few Cairns are actually used these days for hunting or ridding areas of pests, this instinct is an important part of their heritage and temperament.

To earn a Certificate of Gameness, a dog must participate in an American Working Terrier Association Trial. Other certificates are also available for

Four Cairn puppies hunting. This instinct still remains strong in Cairns.

dogs actually used in hunting on a regular basis. The trials, or digs as they are sometimes called, are run in an environment simulating a natural den. While different tunnels are used for beginners on their way to work in the Open class, the only class in which a CG can be earned, the Certificate

of Gameness must be earned in a tunnel 30 feet in length with three 90-degree turns. The handler of the dog may give one command upon release of the dog near the entrance to the tunnel but must remain silent for the rest of the exercise. The dog is timed from the moment he is released. The first part of the score is based on the dog's ability to get through the tunnel to the quarry, a caged rat who at no time is in actual danger of being killed or injured by the dog. The second part of the test is on the dog's ability and willingness to "work" the quarry. Work is defined as barking, whining, growling, scratching, biting, or lunging at the cage. Any definite break in working stops the timing of the dog, even if he starts up again. The dog may exit the tunnel and re-enter it, provided he does not go all the way through the tunnel to the quarry and then back to the entrance again. To qualify, the dog must reach the quarry within 30 seconds, thereby receiving 50 points. Once he reaches the quarry he must not leave it, but must "work" it for a full minute to receive the other 50 points. A dog who successfully earns both sets of 50 points in an Open class has earned his Certificate of Gameness. He may then compete in Certificate classes, comparable to the Best of Breed classes in conformation.

Cairns usually love these trials. For them, it is not work but the chance to do what they were born to do. People, on the other hand, seem to have mixed feelings. Some just do not see the point in having their Cairns run through tunnels underground and bark at caged rats. Others not only enjoy seeing their dogs work to the purpose for which they were bred but actually hunt their dogs in the open. Without exception, the people who actively hunt vermin in the field with their Cairns say that their dogs get along better with other dogs, even males, in a pack situation. Given the fact that most males are territorial and often do not get along with other males unless they are raised together, this is a real plus.

Whether you are a proponent of terrier digs or not, it must be remembered that a cursory look at the Cairn Terrier standard will show clearly that the Cairn Terrier was "designed" to go to ground. He has large, strong teeth set in powerful jaws to defend himself in a fight with his quarry. He has a profuse double coat to protect him from both the weather and the teeth and claws of his adversary.

His body is designed to tunnel into the earth, to turn around underground, and to provide the strength to kill or bolt his prey.

For those interested in working with their Cairns on going to ground, whether for a Certificate of Gameness or just for fun, training can begin in puppyhood. You can start by placing a piece of PVC pipe or other type of pipe approximately 7 or 8 feet long and 8 or 9 inches in diameter in the area where your puppies play. One convenient place is along the fence line of their yard. You can anchor the pipe by tying it to the fence. The natural curiosity of your puppy makes this pipe a natural plaything and soon he will be chasing imaginary mice through it. If you have more than one puppy, they will play endless games of tag over, around, and through the pipe.

If your puppy does not start using the tunnel voluntarily, you can help him by giving him a furry "quarry" to chase. Use a furry mouse toy or a piece of rabbit fur tied to a long string. Tie

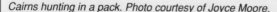
Cairns hunting in a pack. Photo courtesy of Joyce Moore.

a weight such as a heavy washer on the other end of the string. You can put some scent, available through some sporting goods stores or pet supply outlets, on the fur to make it particularly attractive to the puppy. (This works for adults, too.) Then toss the weighted end of the string through the tunnel so that you can grasp the string and pull the scented fur through. Start the fur piece a couple of feet away from the tunnel entrance or have someone toss it about to get the puppy's attention. The puppy or adult will probably not enter the tunnel the first few times you pull the "quarry" through. Never force the issue. Just keep playing, encourage his every move toward the tunnel, and make the training session fun. Keep it short as well. It will take some time for him to work up the courage to go into a dark tunnel if he has not played in it as described earlier.

After he has started regularly chasing the fur through the straight tunnel, add a curve by using an elbow joint and another length of pipe. If you plan to actually hunt your Cairn, you will want to expose him to live game. To start out, you can use laboratory mice bought at a pet store. These mice should be put in a cage that the dog cannot open so he cannot injure them. Allow him to bark, growl, and paw at the cage. Praise him for "working" the mice. Before you know it, he will be ready to go to a Terrier Trial and earn his Certificate of Gameness.

If you would like more information on Terrier Trials, write to the American Working

A Cairn Terrier hunting in the field. Photo by Laura DeVincent.

These five Cairns earned their Certificates of Gameness from the American Working Terrier Association. Photo courtesy of Judy Usafera.

Terrier Association, Rd. 3, Box 254A, Columbia Cross Roads, PA 16914. The friendly people here can also put you in touch with others in your area who compete at the trials or who hunt with their Cairns.

PUPPY TO OLD-TIMER

As your puppy grows, his food needs will change. A good puppy food is fine for the first year, but then an adult maintenance food should be used. Plenty of fresh water is a must at all times. Some Cairns tend to became obese, so do not let your dog overeat. A Cairn should be fairly slender and should have a little dip at his "waistline" between the last rib and the hips. This does not mean, of course, that his ribs should stick out. A healthy, well-fed Cairn will typically have a shine to his coat, a gleam in his eye, and

will be eager to join in any activity that you have planned.

Cairns, like people, change as they age. Depending on the breeding of your puppy, maturity will come any time between a year and a half to three years. Emotional maturity often comes later than physical maturity. Of course, sexual maturity will come as early as six to eight months. Be aware of this if you have an un-neutered or un-spayed Cairn so you do not end up with unwanted puppies. A bitch should never be bred before she is old enough.

Adult Cairns will often retain many of their puppy-like qualities, even into old age. Every Cairn has a distinct personality of his or her own but just about all of them have certain things in common. Many of them will bark at almost anything including settling dust. No one will ever come near your

Mother and son, *Cairnkeep Fiery Teegan* and *Ch. Cairnkeep Call Me Camron*. Photo by Dawn Burdick.

house or apartment without your knowing it. Many Cairns will dig and most will also hunt mice. If you have ever had a cat who presented you with a mouse carcass as a gift, you should not be surprised when your Cairn does the same thing. Cairns and cats have much in common.

Cairns seem to love climbing. They will be all over your furniture if you let them. They will also find a way onto the dining room table, the piano, the window ledges, and whatever else they can reach. Their curiosity draws them into every corner. They will open boxes, crawl into bags, explore the far reaches of your closet, and sleep in open drawers.

A Cairn can own you with one look. If you are not careful, they will soon have you feeding them extra tidbits, taking them for rides in the car, and taking them to the office. They are endearing beyond words.

The average life span of a Cairn is 12 to 14 years. Many will live longer than that. By the time they reach middle age, around eight to ten, they slow down a bit. Now is the time to make sure to keep up those yearly checkups at the vet. Teeth will need extra attention, as plaque seems to build up faster. A change to a senior diet will be in order, as a slower metabolism can cause weight gain. You might notice some silver on the muzzle, especially on a dark dog. Regular exercise is still important and your Cairn will still want to play as if he were a puppy. But you will also find that he sleeps a bit more and seems to value his comfort.

As your Cairn gets older, over ten and into his later years, be sure to pay close attention to his physical and emotional needs. He might be a little cranky now and then, especially if a younger, more energetic dog wants to play and he is just not feeling up to it. Older dogs can get arthritis and creaky joints, just like their owners. Take the extra time to talk to him and pet him. Sometimes a gentle massage can relieve the aches and pains of age as well as enhance emotional well-being.

Hearing and eyesight can start to fail in an older dog. If this is the case, keep his environment as stable as possible. He knows where the furniture is placed and will get around just fine as long as you do not pull any surprises. Be sure that he is warm enough in the winter and cool enough in the summer. His bed should be out of drafts and in a quiet area. If he

Ch. Misty Moor's Wee Nessie and her ten-week-old pups. Photo by Dawn Burdick.

Owning two Cairns is a good idea because they can keep each other company. **Wee Geordie Bit O'Divil** *and* **Clan Macaw Brat's Marigold,** *both at six months old. Photo by Janis Whitcomb.*

sleeps with you, you might eventually have to help him into and out of bed. After the years of devotion he has given you, this is little enough to do for him.

Finally, it is simple logic that your life will be much longer than your Cairn's. Chances are that he will live his life to the fullest, getting the most out of every day, and then in the natural course of things he will die in his bed. However, if he becomes ill and is in pain, the kindest and most loving thing you can do for him is to let him go painlessly and with dignity. This difficult decision can be made with the help of your veterinarian.

When the time comes that his life ends, do not be afraid to grieve for your little friend. It is not strange or abnormal to feel grief at his passing. Your Cairn is not just a dog. He has spent years as a companion, a confidante, and a family member. There are several good books available in the library or through book stores that can help you through this grieving process.

Chances are that in time you will decide that you want another dog. Chances are even better that, having experienced a Cairn Terrier once, you will be compelled to do it again. Somehow, no other breed will do.

Once you have experienced living with a Cairn Terrier—somehow no other breed will do. Owner, Diane M. Blair.

Above:*Ch. Blair Hill Hurricane Emily* out of *Kim-E-Cairns Poor Alfie* x *Ch. Kim-E-Cairn's Hurricane Annie* with a special friend.
Below:*Toto Payne, CD* loves to ride her horse.

136

Above left: *Cairn Terriers love the outdoors, no matter what the weather. Owner, Judy Usefara.* Above right:**U-UD Bonnie Bess, UDT, TDI, CGC** *dressed for pet therapy.* Below: *Words of wisdom from* **Ch. Kirkshire's Spice O'Life** *to* **Kirkshire's Smuggler.**

Winter Wonderland. Above left: **Wee Geordie Bit O'Divil** *and* **Clan Macaw Brat's Marigold** *both at two years of age.* Above right: **Ch. Joywood's Elegant Elise** *and* **Ch. Goosedown's First Edition,** *owned by Pat Hassey.* Below: *Cairns in the snow photographed by Laura DeVincent.*

Wee Geordie Bit O'Divil at 17 months of age. Photo by Janis Whitcomb.

Breeding Your Cairn

ETHICAL CONDUCT

In many countries clubs have adopted a code of ethics with regard to breeding Cairn Terriers. These codes have been established as a guideline for those who wish to consider the welfare of the breed. Anyone, club member or not, who is considering breeding, buying, or selling a Cairn Terrier should read and consider the ethical standards set out by their respective country's clubs.

The following is an example of the requirements of a code of ethics based on one adopted by the Cairn Terrier Club of America. Cairn Terrier breeders will:

1. Conduct themselves at all times in such a manner as to reflect credit on the sport of pure-bred dogs.
2. Keep accurate breeding records, registration papers and pedigrees.
3. Familiarize themselves with the standard of the Breed and strive to breed only dogs and bitches of characteristic type, sound structure and temperament, free of genetically transmitted diseases and faults.
4. Breed no bitch before its second season, and in no event before sixteen (16) months of age, nor more often than two out of three heat seasons, and only then if in robust health.
5. Not continue to breed a Cairn Terrier which has produced one or more offspring in two different litters with a serious defect, or one which would affect the Cairn's health or well-being, especially a defect thought to be genetically linked. An animal with such a condition (i.e. blindness, lameness or impairment of vital organs) will not be sold or otherwise placed for breeding purposes.
6. Not undertake the breeding of a bitch unless they are prepared to keep the resultant puppies until each is suitably placed. Breeders offering a dog at stud should request similar assurances from the owners of outside bitches.
7. Maintain all puppies and

Opposite page: ALL IN THE FAMILY. Top left: **Ch. Cairmar's Leslie,** dam of Ch. Brehannon On The Rocks. Middle left: **Ch. Brehannon On The Rocks,** sire of Ch. Brehannon's Graylan Drummer. Bottom left: **Ch. Brehannon's Graylan Drummer** at two years of age. An important sire in the Brehannon kennel. Top right: **Ch. Brehannon's Demon Drum,** sired by Drummer. Middle right: **Ch. Brehannon's Drum Majorette,** sired by Drummer. Bottom right: **Ch. Brehannon Chocolate Madness,** dam of Drum Majorette.Breeder: Ken Kauffman.

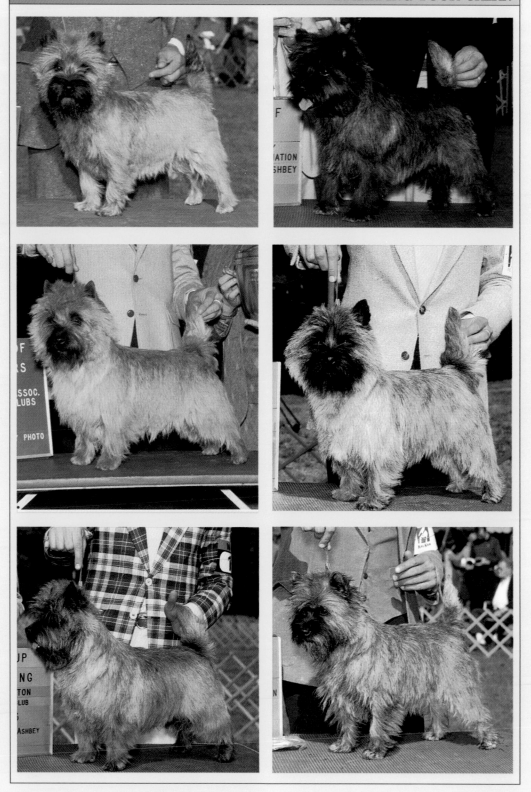

FAMILY PORTRAIT. From left to right: ***Ch. Sharolaine's Kalypso**, sire;* ***Ch. Foxairn Tinman**, son;* ***Ch. Copperglen Foxtrot**, daughter.*

adults in a clean and healthy condition. Puppies shall be at least eight (8) and preferably twelve (12) weeks old before going to a new home. No adult or puppy shall be sold without appropriate inoculations.

8. Not engage in wholesaling or distribution of litters of Cairn Terriers or the selling of breeding stock to such places as pet dealers, catalog houses, or other commercial sources of distribution, nor shall Cairn Terriers be supplied for raffles, lotteries, or laboratory experimentation.

9. Require spaying/neutering of Cairns either with known disqualifying faults, or known to be "carriers of designated genetically linked conditions." In the alternative, breeders shall require and obtain the written consent of the transferee to withhold the registration papers of such an animal until such time as the animal is spayed or neutered, at which time papers may be furnished. Purchasers will be supplied with accurate and valid papers and a pedigree, a registration certificate, a written statement as to whether a guarantee is provided, and will set forth any terms, conditions or limitations thereto, together with complete medical records and instructions for care and feeding.

The importance of adhering to a code of ethics such as this cannot be overemphasized. With anti-dog legislation becoming more prevalent in too many cities and states, every effort must be made by dog owners to be responsible when it comes to breeding dogs.

READ THIS FIRST!

A litter should not ever be conceived without plans already

in place for every puppy. This does not include sales to outlet stores or a trip to the humane society. It means a good home with people who understand their responsibilities to both the puppy and the neighborhood.

Responsible breeders will sell as pets only dogs with strongly worded spay/neuter contracts, who are already spayed/neutered, or who have limited registration certificates. These certificates, while registering the dog or bitch with the American Kennel Club, do not allow the registering of any offspring unless the breeder of the litter requests a change at a later date. Only the breeder can make this change.

People have many reasons for wanting to breed their bitches. Often they mistakenly believe that selling puppies will help them recoup the cost of purchasing the bitch in the first place or perhaps they can earn some extra pocket money by selling puppies. The costs of breeding the bitch such as stud fee, proper nutrition, veterinary care, and possibly complications requiring a Caesarean section (not to mention costs of check-ups, worming, shots, and other care for puppies) add up quickly. Talking to a concerned and ethical breeder about the realities of money spent on producing healthy, sound puppies will put a stop to any thoughts of making big bucks through breeding.

If you have a Cairn who is of breeding quality in both structure and temperament, there are many things to be considered before actually breeding her. First, do you want to take the risk? Most Cairns are easy whelpers and good mothers, but as with anything as traumatic as giving birth, there can be complications. A Caesarean section, when required, can result in death. Not to have the procedure when required will surely end the same way. Eclampsia, or milk fever as it is often called, is a condition that can kill your bitch if she is not treated promptly. Knowing when your bitch is in trouble could save her and her puppies' lives.

Even puppies born alive and well can suffer from any number of problems later. As many as one-third of all puppies of all breeds born do not survive their first two weeks. So before breeding, read a good book or two on the subject and talk to experienced breeders. Make an informed decision with the full knowledge of any risks involved.

Stud dog owners have a responsibility, too. Adding to the dog overpopulation problem by letting an un-neutered dog roam the neighborhood is not good for you or your dog. Breeding a male just so he can have the experience or because a neighbor wants a litter of puppies is only making the problem worse. Dogs should be used at stud carefully and with the same forethought as bitches. Injuries to the dog can occur during breeding, especially if the bitch is not particularly cooperative. Infections that can sterilize a male or make him ill can be transmitted through breeding an infected bitch. Brucellosis is one example.

If you have a dog of either sex, consider that the maxim every true breeder lives by is this: any litter produced should be conceived and bred with the

intent of improving on the parents. This means using a sound bitch with correct breed type and breeding her to the dog who best strengthens her weaknesses, no matter where this dog lives. Of course, this usually means shipping the bitch to another city, possibly clear across the country. Concerned breeders who want to do what is best for the future of the breed will do that. They will do it to have strong, healthy, mentally sound puppies who best exemplify the breed standard whether in the show ring or in your own back yard.

If you have a Cairn that you do not intend to show or breed and who is not already spayed or neutered, it would be a good idea to have this fairly minor surgery done as soon as possible. Spaying or neutering does several things for your dog. For starters, potential health problems associated with the organs involved will be virtually eliminated. A bitch will not go through the estrous, or heat, cycle every six to eight months. This will save her and you the aggravation of having every male in the neighborhood hanging around the back door. Unwanted pregnancy is prevented. Many people feel that males make better pets when they are neutered. Their tendency to roam is lessened and they are less territorial. Males in particular are quite jealous of their territories and will defend them against other males, even those who outweigh them by 100 pounds. To a Cairn male, this territory could be you, your house, or even just a toy. Most important of all, however, is that a neutered male will not contribute to the increasing population of unwanted dogs.

YOU DON'T HAVE TO BE A GENETICIST, BUT...

If, after all due consideration, you decide that you want to go

and the dam. Each parent contributes fifty percent of the genetic material. However, when it comes to physical appearance sometimes the genes from the dam are the ones that show up, and sometimes it is those from the sire. What is important to remember is that every single gene is stored away in your puppy just waiting to be passed on to his offspring, whether it shows up in his own physical characteristics or not.

FAMILY TREE. *Ch. Bonnie Vamp of Wolfpit* on the left with daughter *Ch. Bonnie Tramp of Wolfpit* on the right. Owner, Lydia C. Hutchinson.

ahead and breed your bitch, there are some things you need to know about breeding in general. While you do not need a degree in genetics, you do need some understanding of what goes into producing quality Cairns. A basic understanding of how two plus two doesn't always equal four is important.

Every Cairn is created from a genetic blueprint (remember the standard?) that is a composite of characteristics from both the sire

Some genes are dominant and some are recessive. Dominant genes usually rule the roost, especially when paired with a recessive. Recessive genes are the shy, retiring types who do not like to express themselves unless they are paired together without a dominant in the neighborhood. So if you have a dominant gene for brindle coloring paired with a recessive for wheaten, the brindle gene will take control and your puppy will be brindle. But, if a recessive wheaten gene from the dam pairs with another from the sire, you will have a wheaten puppy from brindle parents. Those pesky little recessive genes can pair to produce something you did not expect.

This is doubly true in areas of health. While Cairn Terriers as a whole are a healthy breed, there are a few problems that have either proven to be inherited or are believed to be. CMO (or Craniomandibular Osteopathy) is one of these. This is a disease that strikes young puppies. Often called Lion Jaw, CMO is a calcification of the bony tissue of the jaw that is painful and occasionally fatal to a puppy who can't use his jaw properly. Early diagnosis and treatment will pull a puppy through but no one would want to breed a Cairn who either had this disease or who produced it in his offspring. Cairns can be carriers of the CMO gene without ever having the disease themselves. Breed a carrier to a carrier and you could get an affected puppy. Breed a carrier to a non-carrier, and you will probably produce more carriers. This is a time-bomb situation. Affected and carrier dogs alike should be neutered or spayed to prevent the gene from

being passed into future generations. The Cairn Terrier breed is lucky not to be plagued with many of the problems associated with other breeds but only vigilance and careful breeding will prevent problems in the future.

THE PLAN

Anyone who is serious about breeding Cairn Terriers should have a plan. You should have an idea of what you want to produce in the puppies that you breed. Breeding for the sake of breeding will get you nowhere. Spend some time looking at as many Cairns as possible to decide what you like and don't like. Then work toward producing what you like. Of course, you want to keep the breed standard and health considerations in mind while you do this.

Many people find that with experience and time their personal preferences in the variations on type can change a bit. This is not unusual nor is it a crime. Constantly redefine your idea of what you want in your Cairns and work toward it.

There are three types of breeding plans to consider when you breed your bitch. The first is outcrossing. This occurs when

Opposite page: THREE GENERATIONS OF CAIRNS. Top left:**Ch. Dapper Dan Of Wildwood,** sire of Fancy Dresser. Middle left: **Ch. Cairmar Fancy That,** dam of Fancy Dresser. Bottom left: **Ch. Cairmar Fancy Dresser** as a young dog. Top right: **Ch. Terriwood's Best Dressed,** a Fancy Dresser son. Middle right: **Ch. Cairland Fast Talker,** a Fancy Dresser son. Bottom right: **Ch. Bramblewood's Cat Dancing,** a Fancy Dresser daughter.

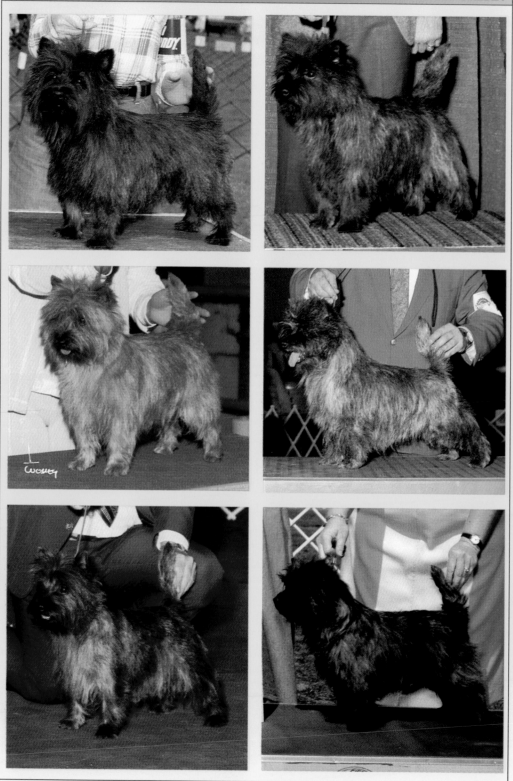

Coat of many colors . . .

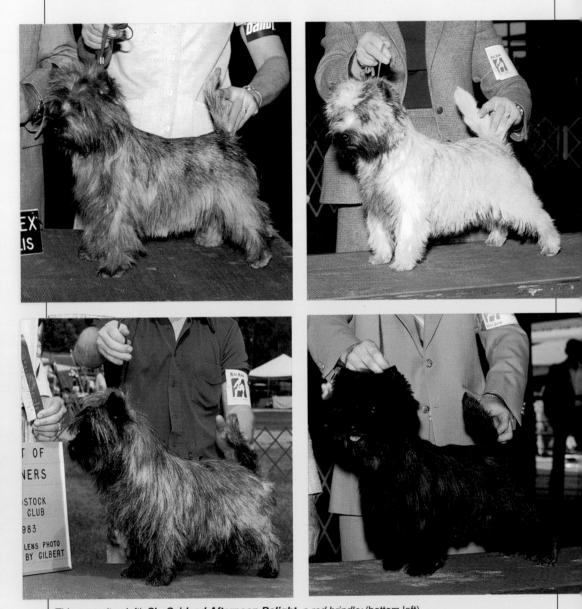

This page: (top left) *Ch. Cairland Afternoon Delight*, a red brindle; (bottom left) *Chasands Trazarra*, a gray brindle; (top right) *Ch. Cairland Highland Delight*, a cream with dark points; (bottom right) *Ch. Cairland Atom Action*, a black brindle.

Opposite page: (top left) *Ch. Cairnkeep Rainstorm*, a silver brindle; (top right) *Ch. Vanessa of Cairmar*, a red; (below) *Ch. Copperglen Foxtrot*, a wheaten with some brindling.

you carefully examine her pedigree and that of her betrothed to find that she has absolutely no relatives anywhere in his pedigree for several generations. Not even cousins! Outcrossing can be valuable in a breeding program, as it brings in new blood, new genetic information that can add vigor to a line or bring in a particular quality you want. Usually when considering an outcross, it is best to find a male whose general appearance is similar to your bitch's. This way, you will have at least a bit of an idea that the resultant puppies might look like mom and dad.

If you do nothing but outcross in your breeding program with no regard to type, your puppies will show it. No two will look like they came from the same litter. Most breeders strive for consistency in their breeding programs. This is not to mean that you can't breed for more neck or more leg, or a shorter tail, but you have to plan to get that result.

The next type of breeding is called linebreeding. This is when the pair to be bred are related, but not too closely. A good example is breeding cousin to cousin or grandfather to granddaughter. The reasoning behind linebreeding is that you narrow down your gene pool and have a better idea of what to expect in your litters. This is especially true if you have done your homework on the lines you are using. By linebreeding, you tend to double up on genes, good and bad. This way you can breed for the good and hopefully breed out the bad, such as soft coats or missing teeth. Take a bitch with many good points who has the fault of a slightly soft coat and breed her to a male in the same line who has complementary good points and a history of a hard coat in both his ancestors and his offspring and you will probably improve the coats on her puppies. In addition, you will double up on the good qualities of both.

The final method used by some breeders is inbreeding. This is the breeding of very close relatives such as mother to son or brother to sister. Inbreeding has its uses. If you want to test-breed for a fault, this is one way to pull it out. If you want to set a certain quality such as a strong front, this is a way to do it quickly.

Opposite page: *FAMILY TIES.* Top left:**Ch. Chasands Travelin' Man**. Middle left: **Chasands Bounty Hunter,** *son of Chasands Travelin' Man.* Bottom left: **Chasands Escape Artist,** *littermate to Chasands Travelin' Man.* Top right: **Ch. Chasands Chantilly Lace.** Middle right: **Ch. Chasands Knight Rider,** *son of Chasands Chantilly Lace.* Bottom right: **Chasands Xanadu,** *littermate to Ch. Chasands Chantilly Lace.*

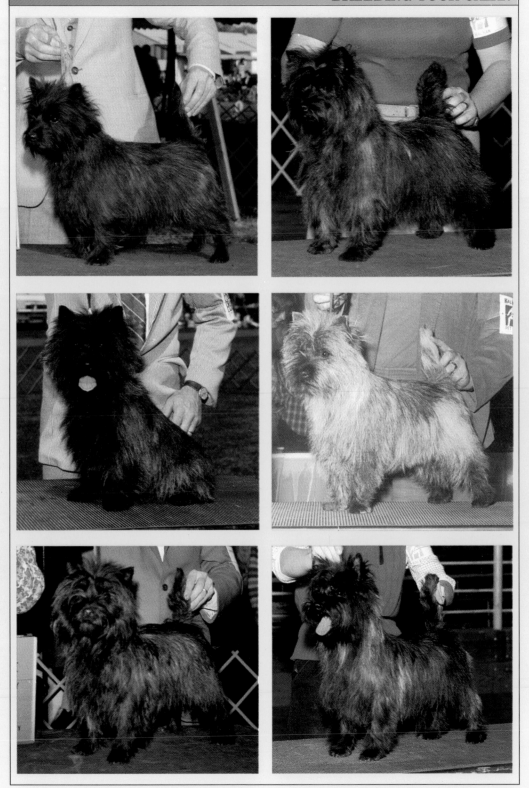

Above: *BLOOD BROTHERS.* (Left) **Ch. Chasands Willie in the Ruff** and (right) **Ch. Chasands This Bud's For You,** *both out of Ch. Rogerlyn Sea Hawks Salty Sam x Ch. Whetstone Miss Dior. Owners, C. and S. LeClair.*

Inbreeding must be used carefully with a full understanding that you will pull out the best and the worst in your sire and dam. While you could produce a prepotent stud or an outstanding show dog from a breeding like this, you could produce every possible fault in your line as well.

Important to note here is the fact that a top show dog is not necessarily a top producing dog. Many people see a widely known show dog and immediately ship off their bitches to be bred to him because of his impressive record. Far more important is looking at what he is producing. A good idea would be to look at his sire and dam and see what else they produced. You might decide to breed to the sire of the top winner rather than the winner himself. While physically he might embody everything good about his own parents, he could be carrying and passing on their faults as well. If the top winner is also producing beautiful puppies and he is a good match for your bitch, go for it.

Many breeders like to linebreed for two generations, then outcross to a similar type of dog for vigor. Others will only outcross or breed "type to type" as they call it. Still others will only linebreed. Whatever you decide to do, remember that you are producing lives for which you are responsible. The future of the breed is in your hands.

CAIRN RESCUE

While on the topic of breeding, we must consider the unfortunate necessity of Cairn Rescue. Cairn Rescue is a coordinated national effort to rescue Cairn Terriers that have been deserted by their owners. Sometimes they are in shelters or found running loose. Occasionally an unscrupulous individual will decide to get rid of breeding stock. Too often they are in bad health with problems ranging from heartworm to malnutrition.

Cairn Rescue volunteers house these Cairns in their own homes or kennels, treating illness and working with rehabilitation if necessary until suitable homes can be found. In some cases, Cairns that are too ill or have temperaments ruined beyond redemption, causing fear biting, or other problems, must be euthanized.

As hard as it is to believe, some Cairns are simply no longer wanted by their human families. Even Cairns with respected kennel names in their backgrounds are not strangers to Cairn Rescue. How does this happen? It happens when we breed and sell puppies without carefully screening potential buyers to make sure that they are serious about our little friends. It happens when we sell a bitch without a limited registration or spay agreement. It happens when we sell an un-neutered dog to someone who decides that a stud fee could come in handy during the holidays. Some of the resultant litter ends up in the pound. It can happen when the owners of a Cairn find his digging habits difficult to cope with, or his barking too annoying.

There are many reasons, but they all come back to our basic

*Rescue Cairns make wonderful, loving housepets. This is **Toto**, a rescue Cairn owned by Betty Vogt.*

responsibility as breeders to take care of our Cairns wherever they might be. If a puppy buyer calls to say he must let his puppy go, it is the breeder's responsibility to take the puppy back and find it a home.

Whether in Great Britain or the United States, national and regional clubs have networks to

stay. If you want a pet and do not necessarily want to take the time to work with a young puppy, a rescue Cairn will give you all the love and companionship you could ever desire. Knowing you helped save this little pal from euthanasia will make him even more valuable to you. A rescue Cairn is only placed when he is of

Toto, a rescue Cairn owned by Betty Vogt, watching outside. He doesn't want to miss anything.

assist in Cairn Rescue. A call to any reputable breeder will connect you with the right person. A rescue Cairn can make a wonderful pet, especially if it is a dog raised in a home where, for a legitimate reason, it can no longer

sound temperament and in good health, often at a price less than that of a cute young puppy. Consider a rescue Cairn as an investment in a life that will repay you many times over.

Somewhere over the rainbow there is a loving home for a rescue Cairn. Before you buy, consider adoption as an option. This rescue Cairn, owned by Cindy Eli, has an obedience title.

Ch. Cairland Airtight Alibi, a handsome red-brindle male in a shaggy coat—before grooming. Photo courtesy of Olin Mills.

Grooming Your Cairn

Grooming a Cairn Terrier, even the fairly painless grooming of a household pet, is a process which takes a while to learn and perfect. Remember that you must be patient both with your Cairn and yourself. If you will recall, you were not too pleased with your mother's early attempts to bathe you and comb the snarls out of your hair!

A beautiful coat does not begin with grooming, or even with a proper diet. It starts with the genes. Dogs with poor coats will tend to produce poor–coated offspring. When you are looking at a litter of puppies, remember this guideline— the adorable puppy with the fluffy coat will probably have a soft, difficult-to-keep coat as an adult. The plain puppy with little or no fluff will probably have the correct hard coat when he grows up. Pet or show quality, a Cairn's coat should be hard without being coarse, shiny with health, and dense. It should be straight, although a slight wave is allowed, and should lie fairly close to the body. Your best bet is to simply purchase a puppy bred from parents with good coats. Your chances of a good coat on your newfound friend will be better.

There is some truth to the saying that wheatens have softer coats overall than Cairns of other colors. Some reds and brindles have coats so hard that it is almost impossible to keep leg and head furnishings of any length. If this short coat is not what you desire, you can put oil preparations, available at many pet product stores, on the furnishings. Some moisturizers meant for human hair work just as well but make sure they contain nothing hazardous to your dog's health if he decides he likes the tasty treat on his whiskers or legs.

Proper feeding is vital to maintaining what nature has given your puppy. Nothing will lay a good coat to waste faster than generic dog food. A high-quality food is all that is needed. In fact, supplementing with various vitamins, powders, and other touted preparations can throw off the balance of the ingredients so carefully achieved in the food you have purchased.

When it comes to actual grooming, brushing often with a natural bristle brush and keeping toenails clipped short are two of the best things you can do for your puppy. Daily brushing gets your puppy used to handling and offers the added benefit of close contact with you. Gently brushing and stroking the pup at the same time makes this an enjoyable experience for both of you.

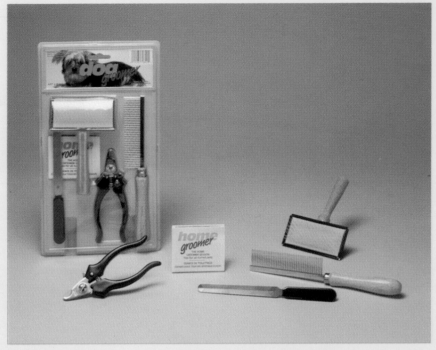

In order to ensure that you have everything you need for the daily grooming of your dog, pick up a grooming kit from your local pet-supply store. Photo courtesy of Hagen.

NAIL TRIMMING

Nail clipping is not pleasant but it is absolutely necessary in order to prevent breakdown of the pastern. If nails are allowed to grow too long, two things can happen. The first, and potentially most painful, is that they will curl under the dog's feet eventually cutting into the pads themselves, causing extreme pain. The second, although not as obvious, is just as serious. Long nails push the weight of the foot farther back than nature meant it to be, causing the foot to bend in an unnatural position. This breaks down the pastern, the area just above the foot, weakening the entire leg structure. This can cause limping, uncomfortable movement, and injury.

To clip the puppy's nails, grasp the foot and gently squeeze a toe at its base so that it will separate from the others for easy access. Using doggie-toenail clippers, snip off the end of the toenail. You can see how far back to cut by looking at the underside of the nail. There is a groove that runs from the end of the toenail to just past the quick. Clip as close to the quick as possible, then file the nail smooth. If you do nick the quick, don't panic. Preparations for stopping any bleeding are available and work quickly. Weekly or bi-weekly nail clipping will become routine for both you and your Cairn if you do not let his tendencies to become a dramatic actor performing a death scene get to you.

BATHING

Bathing the Cairn is to be discouraged unless he is really filthy or has gotten into something that makes him an unacceptable house guest. Unfortunately, any Cairn who has the chance to roll in something totally disgusting will take every opportunity to do so. Bathing too often can dry out a Cairn's skin and soften the coat. A better alternative is to dampen a towel with warm water and vigorously rub your dog down with it, then dry him with a clean towel. A blow-dryer comes in handy—set on medium, not hot— to finish drying the Cairn so that he does not become chilled. There are also waterless shampoos available at commercial outlets and dog shows that can be sprayed on the offending areas, rubbed in, and then toweled dry.

TEETH

Teeth also need attention. Chewing proper doggie toys and treats can help keep teeth clean and breath fresh. There are a great variety of Nylabone® products available that veterinarians recommend as safe and healthy for your dog or puppy to chew on. These Nylabone® Pooch Pacifiers® usually don't splinter, chip, or break off in large chunks; instead, they are frizzled by the dog's chewing action, and this creates a toothbrush-like surface that cleanses the teeth

and massages the gums. Occasionally, however, plaque will build up and need to be removed professionally. If you notice your dog's breath has a bad odor, check his teeth for brown or yellowish plaque. If the problem has become more advanced, his gums will look red and inflamed instead of healthy and pink. Your veterinarian will perform a complete teeth cleaning for a moderate price. Brushing the teeth regularly with a piece of gauze wrapped around your finger or a soft toothbrush using specially made dog toothpaste is recommended as a preventive. Do not use human toothpaste. It will upset your dog's stomach.

EARS

Ears, too, need periodic cleaning. Pre-moistened wipes are

You can find many safe dog shampoos at your local pet shop. Photo courtesy of Hagen.

available at pet supply outlets, or a warm washcloth can be used to clean the visible portions of the inside ear. Long hairs should be removed from the insides of the ears to help keep them clean. If you notice your Cairn shaking his head often or scratching at the inside of his ears, he might have ear mites. These should be treated by your vet with specially medicated drops.

BASIC GROOMING

If you are one of those people who wants more than a shaggy little haystack running around the house, a couple of hours a month will give you a dog who looks like a proper Cairn. While Cairns do not actually shed much top coat, undercoat is shed twice a year, especially in the spring. Vigorous brushing helps keep this shedding to a minimum.

The first thing to do is to obtain the right equipment to groom your pet. You will need a brush, a metal comb, scissors, thinning shears, and if you are really serious about keeping a male tidy, electric clippers for the genital area.

Start by thoroughly brushing your dog. Tell him often what a good boy he is. Clip his nails and get that task out of the way immediately. Then trim the hair from the bottom of his feet with the scissors. This will not only give him better traction, but in the winter it will prevent ice balls from building up between his toes. Placing his foot back down on the grooming table or whatever is passing for one, scissor his feet into a round shape when viewed from above. Thinning shears can neaten the feet and cover up the scissor marks.

Gumabone® products come in a variety of colors and shapes and have been proven to reduce the buildup of calculus in dogs.

AmCan. Ch. Terriwood's Mighty Legacy —scruffy but tidy. Owners, Tom and Karin Godwin.

Next, the ears need to be trimmed. Taking a few hairs at a time firmly between your thumb and forefinger, pull them out completely. You only want to "strip" out the hair from the top one–third of the ear. You may use scissors to even up the edges to a nice point, but be careful. Once nicked, twice shy as the saying goes. If pulling out hair by the roots sounds too painful (actually it isn't), you can carefully lay the scissors flat against the upper third of the ear and cut the hair off. You will need to use one finger as a base to lay the ear against, then press with the flat of the scissors.

The rest of the body, legs, and tail can be trimmed to the desired length using thinning shears or clippers with a blade guard for a half-inch hair length. Just follow the natural body contours with whichever tool you choose. Do use the thinning shears on the tail, which should be shaped like an inverted carrot with a point at the end. The genital area of males can be clippered to keep it clean, but caution is recommended to avoid

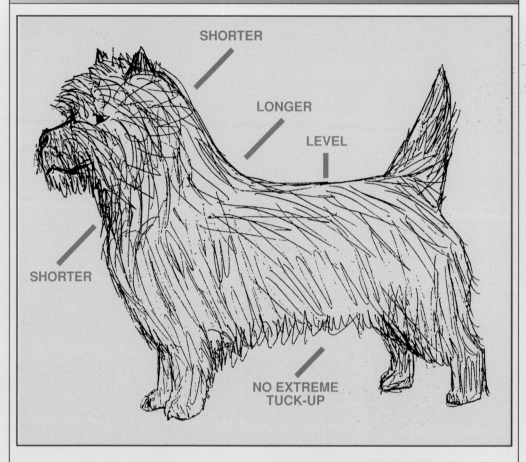

SHORTER

LONGER

LEVEL

SHORTER

NO EXTREME TUCK-UP

clipper burns or nicks.

Remember that any cutting of the coat will soften it. This is due to the way hair grows on a Cairn. The first 2 inches of hair growing out of a follicle is hard, the proper texture. As the hair continues to grow, the new portion near the skin comes out of the follicle softer and thinner. When the hair is cut, the hard end is removed leaving only the softer, silkier hair. The more it grows, the softer it gets. Only by removing the hair from the follicle and allowing a brand new hair to formulate and grow is the coat kept hard.

STRIPPING THE COAT

If you want to be more of a purist, you can strip your dog down completely every six or eight months and just let the hair grow out evenly all over. Stripping a dog means pulling the top coat completely out by hand and letting it start over from scratch. By the time a hair is three or four inches long, it is very loose in the follicle and ready to come out. Simply grasp a few hairs at a time and with a quick wrist-snapping action, pull them out. If you do not grip too tightly, any hair that is not ready to come out easily will slip through your fingers.

Obviously, stripping an entire dog takes time. Most Cairns, not to mention their owners, are tired out before the entire job is done. It is suggested that stripping be done over a period of several days or even a few weeks. Start with the head and leg furnishings. Then progress to the sides, tail, neck, and back.

If you want to combine stripping and using the thinning shears, strip the top of the neck, the back, and about halfway down the sides of the dog. Then use the thinning shears on the rest of the neck, sides, belly, legs, and tail. You will end up with hard coat on the back and generally longer, softer hair everywhere else. Your

Cairn will appreciate your not stripping his entire head, as this is a sensitive area.

GOING TO A PROFESSIONAL GROOMER

The easiest way to groom your Cairn is to let someone else do it. Most grooming shops will clipper your Cairn for a moderate price. However, it will probably look more like a Miniature Schnauzer, a most un-Cairn-like appearance. It is possible to find a professional groomer who knows how to strip a terrier, but the cost is usually prohibitive because of the time and work involved.

Sometimes a local Cairn breeder and exhibitor will groom

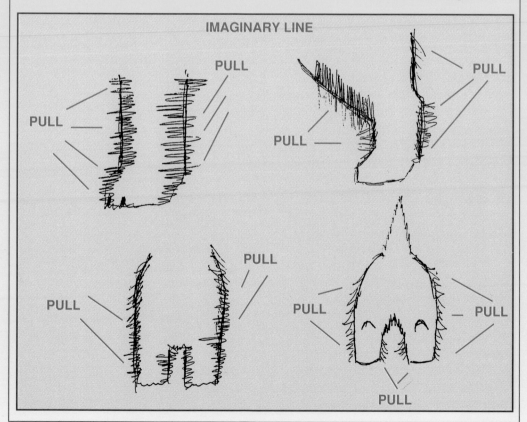

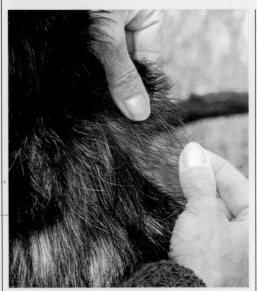

To strip your Cairn's coat, roll a little coat up between your thumb and forefinger and then pull out the longer hairs. Photo by Jack De Witt.

your dog for you. The price will vary. Do remember that most serious breeder/exhibitors have their own show dogs to keep in coat, a very time consuming venture, and therefore might not be able to groom for anyone else. However, many will be glad to assist you in learning how to do it yourself.

GROOMING THE SHOW DOG

Anyone looking at a show ring full of Cairn Terriers in all of their full-coated glory should be impressed by how natural they look. There should be no exaggerated heads, looking more like West Highland White Terriers than proper Cairns. Tails should be carrot shaped, not resembling the "stove-pipe" tails of the Fox Terrier or the Scottie. Toplines should be level. Bottom lines

should also be fairly level with only a bit of "tuck-up" and certainly no scissoring to give the look of the Miniature Schnauzer. Moderate is the word used throughout the standard and grooming should follow that instruction.

Of course, one does not want to see a show dog with a dirty or untidy coat either. Long, dead hair or fly-away coats are just as incorrect as those overly done.

It is amazing how much work goes into making a Cairn look tidy and scruffy at the same time. This look is achieved by starting coat care by the time the puppy is eight to 12 weeks old and keeping up with it every week thereafter. After the basics of proper breeding for good coats, nutrition, brushing, and nail trimming are taken care of, the real work begins.

Stripping the Puppy Coat

The correct Cairn coat should be "built." When the puppy's fluffy baby coat is looking loose, usually by the age of three months, it should be gently pulled out—all of it. Grasping a few hairs at a time between thumb and forefinger and using a snapping wrist action, pull it out quickly. It helps to slightly stretch the skin in the opposite direction from the way you are pulling. This makes the hair come out easier and lessens any discomfort to your puppy. You can chalk your dog before pulling, as this sometimes makes the coat easier to grip. Dead hair comes out easily and will not hurt the pup as you pull it. It is okay to leave the hair on the muzzle around the nose and lips as playing with littermates usually takes care of it. If not, pull this out, too. Puppy will not appreciate your efforts on his behalf, so give him lots of pets and praise. A treat or two certainly won't hurt either.

Rolling the Coat

From puppyhood clear into adulthood, at least once a week go over the entire puppy pulling out any loose hair. There are several ways to do this. One is to brush the hair against the grain and pull out any long hair. Another method is to start at the tail and thigh area and gently roll a narrow strip of hair up between your left thumb and forefinger (if you are right-handed, that is). Then with your right hand, pull long or loose hairs out of that thin line. These will be pretty obvious as they will stick out longer than the rest of the hair. Moving forward a fraction of an inch, repeat the process until the entire back, both sides, and neck are done. You can also simply lift a small section of coat with your fingers and pull out any loose strands of hair.

The legs are done by gently

Before and after. **Tanglevines Sydmonton** *before being stripped of fluffy puppy coat* (above) *and after being stripped* (below). *Note the dark points that were hidden under his fluff. Owner, Carolyn Myers.*

combing the hair straight out from the leg and pulling out loose or long hair all the way around to make the leg look roughly like a fence post. Care should be taken not to "post" the leg to the extreme that it looks like a Wire Fox Terrier leg. It is necessary to keep the shaggy look while tidying

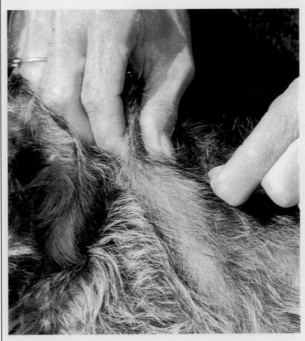

When stripping your Cairn, pull the skin back to pick at the coat without hurting the dog. Photo by Jack DeWitt.

coats on puppies clear through the first years of their lives this way without ever having to completely strip the coat. The secret is to start young and stay on top of it. This means grooming at least once every seven to ten days.

The Art of Grooming for Show

Now you have a young adult whose coat has been properly cared for since puppyhood and you want to shape it for the show ring. You have several layers of coat already starting to show, which adds volume and thickness, but it is too long on parts of the dog and not long enough on others. The dog does not have the balanced, tidy look of those you have seen winning the blue ribbons. This is where the "art" of grooming comes into play.

First you must have a picture in your mind of what the ideal Cairn Terrier should look like. For most exhibitors, not to mention judges, this will be a balanced dog somewhat longer than tall with a tidy yet scruffy coat of medium length, at least two inches or more. There should be full coat on the head, an arching neck sloping into well laid-back shoulders and continuing into a dead-level topline. A perfectly set tail of no greater length than the top of the ears when both are held erect will

up the coat.

On the tail it might be easier to use a stripping knife, again pulling out only loose hair. Be sure to get proper instruction on how to use a knife so as not to cut the coat. Using a dulled stripping knife is preferable to one with a sharp cutting edge for just pulling out coat.

This entire process, called rolling a coat, will open up hair follicles to start new growth after a period of dormancy. The result should be new hair of varying lengths growing in at all times, leading to the so-called perfect coat with one layer prime, another layer just ready to be pulled off, and a new layer coming on strong just under the prime coat. Many breeders have successfully rolled complete the topline picture. Of course, this tail is the proper inverted carrot shape. Legs should be fully furnished without hair flopping up and down during movement, and the proper moderate angulation will be apparent both at the shoulder and at the bend of stifle and well-let down hock. Feet will be tight,

the person doing the work. For our purposes here, the descriptions will begin with the feet and move upward on the legs to the sides of the dog, then up to the neck, over the shoulders and back, and on down to blend with the legs. Head and tail will be left for last to match the rest of the dog.

Ch. Cairland Airtight Alibi after show grooming and in a "new," somewhat short coat.

round, and the dog will stand well up on his toes. What a pretty picture!

Now, since most exhibitors do not have this perfect Cairn, they must set out to achieve the most positive picture they can with the Cairn they do have. Grooming the various parts of the Cairn into the perfect whole can be done in whatever order is most logical to

Feet

First, trim the nails if that has not yet been done. They should be kept very short to keep the pads tight and the pasterns strong. Round, compact feet with arched toes and thick pads are the perfect base upon which to build your picture. Next, during one of the few times you will be allowed to get scissors anywhere near your Cairn, trim the hair from between the pads on the bottom of the foot and cut the hair very close to the bottom of the foot on the back and sides. Do not trim the longer hair growing from the top of the foot or higher up on the sides of the feet. Only trim around the pads themselves. Picture the foot as it bears the weight of the dog. It should be circular in shape as if it were the bottom of a post. Now, hold the leg. Using thumb and forefinger, pull out excess hair from the side and top of the foot being careful not to pull too much. Shape the foot so that no long hairs hang in lumps and clumps off the sides or front. When combed down, the hair should cover the foot, forming a circle on the table. It should be trimmed close on the sides and should cover the nails in front. By constantly pulling just a little hair all over the foot, you will build a thick coat.

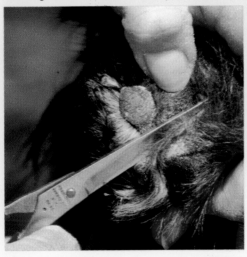

Trimming between the toes. Photo by Jack De Witt.

Front Legs

Moving up the legs facing the dog from the front, comb the hair or pull it away from the leg with your fingers so that it stands straight out from the leg on the sides. Now, picture an imaginary line on the inside of the leg from the ground up to the chest starting at the inside of the foot where the hair should stand out just a little bit. Any hair that sticks out past that imaginary line should be pulled. Do not use scissors or thinning shears as it will not only make the leg look scissored, but will soften and thin the coat in the long run. Pulling will constantly keep new coat coming in, giving a thicker appearance to the leg furnishings.

Do the same imaginary line and pulling of hair on the outside of the leg to the elbow and even part of the way up the shoulder. This will give you a straight leg when viewed from the front. Now move around to the side of your dog and do the same thing on the front and back of the leg. By keeping the line in your mind and visualizing it on the leg, you will see where hair needs to grow longer or needs to be pulled to make that leg look straight. By pulling a bit, then combing the hair down, you can see if you are getting the effect you want. Keep at it until the leg gives the appearance of dropping straight from the chest and shoulder. You will need to then pull the hair out from the shoulder and blend it into the line of the leg for a clean

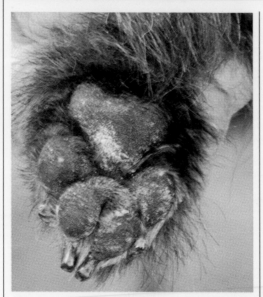

Bottom view of properly trimmed foot. Photo by Jack De Witt.

look. Make sure that the hair at the elbow does not stick out. Have someone move the dog toward you to see if more hair needs to come off of that area.

Rear Legs

Do the rear legs exactly the same as the front legs up to the hock joint. Then you need to groom the bend of the stifle to the shape you desire by again using an imaginary line, this time curved to the correct bend, and pulling out hair that protrudes beyond this line. Thigh hair on the flat of the leg should be full without being too fluffy. This can be rolled to maintain shape, length, and thickness. The back of the thighs under the tail and to the top of the hock joint should be a neat inverted "V." Hair should be kept clear of the anus, but do

not clipper that area, as it ruins the natural look of the dog. Scissors used judiciously very close to the anus are acceptable to keep hair free from this area. Some people will use thinning shears to keep the hair from the back of both thighs, between the anus and vulva or testicles, shorter and thinned so that it does not present a bulky or lumpy appearance when the dog is viewed from the side with his tail up. While pulling this hair out is to be preferred from a theoretical standpoint, it can be painful to your dog, as this is obviously a sensitive area. Be warned, however, that using thinning shears here will result in hair that sticks almost straight out as it grows.

Back, Neck, and Sides

Now blend the hair using the rolling technique from the thighs up onto the back to just a couple

Outside view of properly trimmed foot. Photo by Jack De Witt.

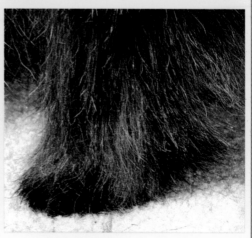

of inches in front of the tail. Lift up a section of coat between left thumb and forefinger and pluck out the long or loose strands. Use this sectioning method for the entire coat. Often the hair on the dog's back just in front of the tail will be thicker than elsewhere on the body and needs to be pulled more heavily to keep the topline level. When you have finished with the thighs and the back section in front of the tail, move to the top of the neck and groom back towards the tail. In order to have the pretty sloping neck, keep the hair at the top of the neck a little shorter, graduating to longer hair at the base of the neck so that the tips of the longest hair just reach past the withers. This gives a smooth and unbroken line to the neck and improves the look of shoulder layback. Pull more coat on the back of the dog than on the sides, blending the coat down to the side furnishings going from shoulder to loin where you meet the area already groomed. Then go back to the neck and pull the front and sides of it to blend in with the rest of the dog. If you pull *slightly* more hair on the front of the neck just under the jaw to about one-third or one-half of the way down the chest in a "V" shape, you will add the illusion of length to the neck. Whatever you do, do not pull so much that your dog looks like a Westie. Coat length should be a minimum of 2 inches overall on the neck, back, and sides.

Tail

The tail should be rolled along with the rest of the coat to continue building it. It should look like an inverted carrot, not a stovepipe. Usually hair is kept longer on the front side of the tail, especially if it has a slight curve,

Side view of front leg before trim. Photo by Jack De Witt.

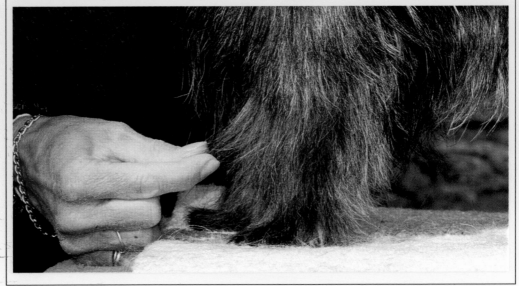

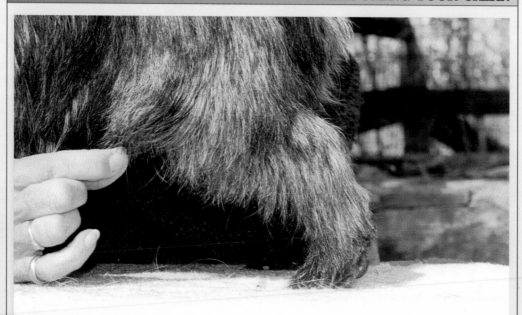

Side view of back leg before trim. Photo by Jack De Witt.

and a bit shorter on the back. Feathering is not acceptable. The tail should have a broad base and should gradually narrow to the pointed tip. Hand plucking or using a stripping knife will give the best finish. Some groomers use thinning shears on the very tip if they do not have the skill with the stripping knife that is required to do the job.

Head

A Cairn's head is the most difficult area to groom. Of course, it is also one of the most important since the Cairn Terrier expression is so important to breed type. The first thing to do is to picture the shape of the head as a rough circle when faced head-on. Brush the hair upward and forward, then stand back to see what hair falls outside of your imaginary circle. Pull this hair out. This will mainly consist of the hair on the very top of the head between the ears and down the back side of the head behind the jaw and then on the underside of the jaw. Many people will leave too much hair clumped just behind the hinge of the jaw or the mandibular joint. Make sure this area is cleaned out of enough hair to keep the head looking round when viewed from the front. Sometimes it helps to blow gently into your dog's ears to get him to shake his head. There is no better way to see how his head coat will look in the ring where he is sure to shake out your careful combing the minute the judge looks his way.

Next, comb the hair on top of the head down over the eyes and picture a visor protecting them from the sun. This visor should extend almost to the nose in the center. Pull out any hair extending beyond the edge of the imaginary visor from ear to ear. Now brush everything up and forward again and pretend you are shaping a pom-pom with the hair from the visor to the top of the head. In order to increase the perception of more stop, even if there is plenty there, pull a small amount of coat very short between the eyes at the stop. It will grow out shorter than the visor hair, giving the look of an excellent stop underneath shaggy brows.

If you have not done so already, shorten the hair under the lower jaw to match the circle you have already formed around the head. Then brush the hair on the muzzle forward and circle the jaw with your left hand (if you are right handed). Brush the hair straight out so that it stands at a 90-degree angle from its roots and again picture the inevitable circle around the muzzle and pull out any hair sticking out of those boundaries. Comb the hair down and view the jaw line from the side. You want to see the bottom line of the jaw fairly level almost all the way to the beginning of the neck. Pull out any hair hanging down too far.

To finish off the top of the muzzle, firmly holding the hair on the bottom of the muzzle, comb the hair on the top in a "snowplow" direction back toward the eyes. There will be a part down the center of the muzzle to

the nose and some hair will probably cover the eyes as you comb it back. Pull out that eye-covering hair. This will give your dog the bright-eyed look you want without taking too much hair off the top of the muzzle.

Brush the head forward and upward again, pulling out any hair on the cheeks or elsewhere that does not look as if it fits in with the picture. It takes time to develop an eye for this.

If it is possible, have someone who really knows how to groom do one side while you observe, then you do the other to match.

Ears

Keep the top one-third of the ears pulled down to velvet or undercoat and graduate the length of the rest of the ear hair to correspond with the circle you have groomed around the head. It is preferred to hand strip the ears instead of using scissors, although this is one place that you can sharpen the outline with scissors if necessary.

Always keep in mind that you are grooming a Cairn, not a Westie. Never use scissors or thinning shears on the head, neck, body, or legs of your dog. The only exceptions are the tip of the ears, tip of the tail, around the foot pads, and around the anus. The underline should be kept up with a stripping knife if it is touched at all.

The end result of all of this work is a Cairn Terrier who looks properly scruffy but tidy, who has a minimum of three layers to his coat, and who will be able to compete with any other dog in the ring as far as correct grooming is concerned. Resist the urge to take shortcuts such as scissoring. The scissor marks are obvious to an experienced eye and will eventually destroy the hard texture of the coat as the healthy ends are cut off. If you work on your dog a minimum of once every week, you will spend only 20 minutes to an hour each time and will have a coated terrier you will be proud to take into any show ring.

PATTERN STRIPPING AND FAULT GROOMING

Pattern stripping and fault grooming are progressive subjects. It is suggested that grooming basics be soundly learned before trying these, although exhibitors who have had experience with other coated breeds will probably be ready to try them as soon as the coat is ready. Purists will argue that while pattern stripping might be acceptable, fault grooming is not.

It must also be remembered that there are different kinds of coats. Some are hard, grow in layers, and have sufficient undercoat without possessing so much that you must constantly dig it out. Others are soft and no amount of grooming will make them hard. Still others resist rolling and will only respond to total stripping, making any scheduling of shows difficult at

Kim-E-Cairn's Chassy Lassie owned by Janet M. Nissen.

best. Too much undercoat is a problem for certain lines. It must simply be laboriously grubbed out with a rake or a dull stripping knife inch by inch. This is a lot of work! Not enough undercoat is a problem, especially in warmer climates. Most judges will forgive a lack of undercoat in the hot months of summer, but will certainly look for it in the cooler months since it is required by the standard.

Pattern Stripping

There are two types of pattern stripping. The most commonly used is diagramed for your study. Pattern stripping is simply first pulling out the area of coat that tends to grow the slowest, then at

Above:***Wee Geordie Bit O'Divil*** and ***Clan Macaw Brat's Marigold*** *both at two years of age. Photo by Janis Whitcomb.* Opposite page: ***Ch. Bramblewood's BMW*** *at 18 months of age. Owned by Glenna Barnes. Photography by Don Petruliso.*

a later date pulling out a different area that grows slightly faster and so on. This allows the coat when fully grown to have a head start on giving the proper picture to an observer. For example, leg and head furnishings are pulled out first as they typically grow very slowly. The coat on the back grows quite quickly. If it were pulled at the same time as the legs and head, the back would be in full show coat long before the other areas were ready. A Cairn with thick coat on his back and toothpick legs along with a practically hairless head would make a strange sight indeed. If you then pulled out the back coat again, before long you would have a Cairn with shaggy legs and head and a back coat that was too short to match.

As you can see from the diagram, you first pull out the head and leg furnishings. On some Cairns, this coat will take up to six months to grow to proper length. Leg coat is to be shorter than body coat and is to be hard in texture. By rolling the coat as it grows, you will add volume and thickness. The newly growing hair pushes the older hair up and out for this effect.

Several weeks after legs and head are pulled, the sides and the base of the tail should be pulled. These grow quicker than the legs and head but not as fast as the back and neck. A few weeks later, pull the front of the neck and chest and the rest of the tail. Also pull about half or more of the coat

where the neck slopes down over the withers. Just pull the hair on top of the dog here and go slightly past the withers. Leave some coat there to pull later for added volume.

Last but certainly not least, pull the back and the rest of the neck. Some people like to take ten days to two weeks between each session, but timing really depends on how fast your dog grows coat. Some will work perfectly on this bi-weekly schedule. Others will take much longer on legs and head, then the time between the rest of the areas to be stripped can be shortened. Only experience with a particular dog will let you know what timing to use.

The other type of pattern stripping is not often used but works well if done properly. This involves stripping out approximately one-third of the coat over the entire body of the dog at once. This includes legs, head, tail, body, everything. Then wait for approximately one month and take out another third of the coat. By now your Cairn will look pretty awful. He will be partly naked with strands of long hair lying listlessly against his body or floating gently in the breeze. Grit your teeth and bear it for another

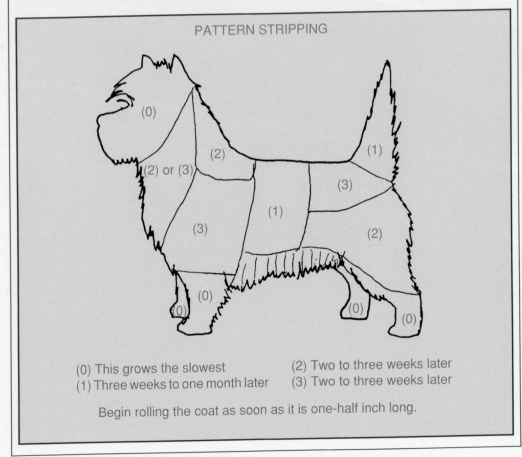

PATTERN STRIPPING

(0) This grows the slowest (2) Two to three weeks later
(1) Three weeks to one month later (3) Two to three weeks later

Begin rolling the coat as soon as it is one-half inch long.

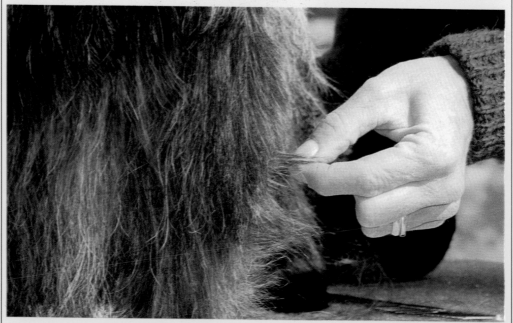

Front view of front leg before trim. Photo by Jack De Witt.

month. Then remove the rest of his coat completely.

By using this method, you have gotten a head start on building three layers of new coat. As the coat comes in, it will be in three lengths, each just slightly shorter than the first. Once it is an inch or so in length, you can start rolling it in the pattern described under pattern stripping. Notice that you roll it, not strip it. You roll the back more heavily, as you want that coat shorter than the sides or head.

When the top layer of coat reaches a length that is too long, you can pull it completely off and you will find that there are two good layers of coat under it from your initial stripping as well as some new coat coming in from your regular rolling efforts. A dog

bred for good coat who is kept up by weekly or bi-weekly grooming sessions will rarely have to be stripped again.

Fault Grooming

Fault grooming is a sensitive subject. Many exhibitors and breeders believe that a dog with faults obvious enough to need to be groomed out should not be shown at all. Others believe that since there is no such thing as a perfect Cairn, one should not throw the baby out with the bath water and that it is an exhibitor's responsibility to show a dog to its best advantage.

Of course, any dog with major faults or too many minor ones should be spayed or neutered and sold as a pet. Some breeders use the "strike three, you're out" rule.

Any dog with three faults they consider minor but bothersome is considered pet-quality. For example, a dog with a bit of a light eye who also has a short upper arm and a tail set a wee bit low would qualify for three strikes.

Fault grooming absolutely does not include surgical correction of a fault such as monorchidism or a gay tail. It also does not include such practices as artificially coloring a dog. These practices are not only illegal in the dog show ring but are unethical as well.

This section on fault grooming is to help the exhibitor present his dog well. It is up to the breeders not to sell dogs who are substandard as show quality animals and up to exhibitors to show only those Cairns who truly deserve to be in the ring.

While there are as many ways to fault-groom a dog as there are faults, this section will cover the basics that are most often found in the dogs. While some exhibitors are experts at creating the illusion of a perfect dog by grooming to increase the look of shoulder layback or bend of stifle, most are better off taking care of the obvious. Time and experience will bring the more esoteric methods to light.

HEADS

There are several head faults found in today's Cairn Terriers. Too long a muzzle or one that is snipey is often found in conjunction with a skull that is too narrow. Often the stop is not as abrupt or deep as it should be.

The best way to add more stop is to pull at a small section of coat between the eyes just barely above the beginning of the actual stop. This should be done several weeks after the rest of the head coat has been rolled or pulled. The resulting shorter hair will tend to stand straight out, giving the appearance of a strong stop, especially when the brow coat is combed down over the eyes.

To shorten that long muzzle, roll the muzzle hair so that it is as full as possible. Remember that new coat just pushing out of the follicle will push the longer hair covering it up and out, giving the illusion of thickness. Also let the visor hair or brow grow longer than you normally would. It should reach the nose when combed down. Then be sure than you comb it well forward over the eyes. The hair to the sides of the eyes and the cheeks should also be brushed well forward. It is amazing how much this will shorten any muzzle. These methods and letting the hair on the bottom of the jaw grow a tad longer than normal will also take care of a snipey muzzle.

A skull that is too narrow usually can be broadened by a full coat of head hair. Keep it as short as possible under the chin and lower jaw. Rather than a perfect circle, let the sides, especially from the middle of the ear to the mandibular joint, grow a little longer than the top or bottom.

Ears that are too large should

be kept closely trimmed. Instead of only trimming the top third of the ear, trim it halfway down and let the head hair around it grow profusely. Be sure to pull the hair out by hand instead of using any scissors, even on the tips or upper edges. Pulling encourages darker hair to grow and dark ears look smaller than light ones.

Ears that are too round on the tips can be sharpened by using scissors but only at the tip.

NECK

A neck that appears too short will be helped by letting the hair on the top of the neck to the withers grow longer than the sides and front. You want this hair graduated in length with the shortest hair near the ears and the longest hair over the withers.

Pull more hair from the sides of the neck, being careful to blend it with the top. From the area where the lower jaw meets the neck to the middle of the chest, keep the hair fairly short. Be sure not to take it down to the extreme of a Westie but do keep it shorter than the sides or the top. This adds the illusion of neck length.

When you are stacking your dog, keep the lead well up under the jaw and pull the neck upward. Do not stretch the neck out forward, as it only throws the picture of the dog completely out of balance.

TOPLINE

There is not much you can do about a roached topline except place the dog as a pet. However, for a slight dip behind the withers there is hope. Roll that area heavily at first to build up more coat, always leaving some long hair to smooth over the top. This will take care of a slight dip. During exhibition, constantly check this area and use a comb to lift the coat over the dip when necessary. At the same time, keep the area from the middle of the back (where the dip goes back up to normal) to the base of the tail groomed short. A really bad topline should qualify the dog for a wonderful house pet.

TAIL

The desired tail is fairly short and straight. When held erect, its tip should be the same height as the tips of the ears. There is not much to do with a tail that is too long. Making sure that it is the proper carrot shape with a broad base narrowing to a pointed tip will help. A tail that is too short is easy to remedy. Simply let the hair grow longer than the tip of the tail and put its end where necessary. Few Cairns have this problem.

A curving tail is more of a challenge. A long, banana-shaped tail is undesirable in any event. Sometimes, although not always, this indicates problems in the real assembly. The best method of grooming is to keep the hair on the front of the tail longer to fill in some of the curve and keep the hair on the back as short as possible to minimize the curve.

Feathering on the tail is always unacceptable, as is a gay tail that curves over almost touching the back.

A somewhat low-set tail can be helped by building up the coat just in front of it and at the base to give the appearance of proper set-on. However, if the dog holds his tail straight out behind him instead of upright, no amount of grooming will cover the set of it.

LEGS

A dog who is out at the elbow is unfortunately too common a sight. This can be helped by keeping the hair pulled very close at the elbow, on the back, and the side near the back of the point of the joint. Pulling too much hair from the side as viewed from the front will only accentuate the problem.

Crooked legs can be

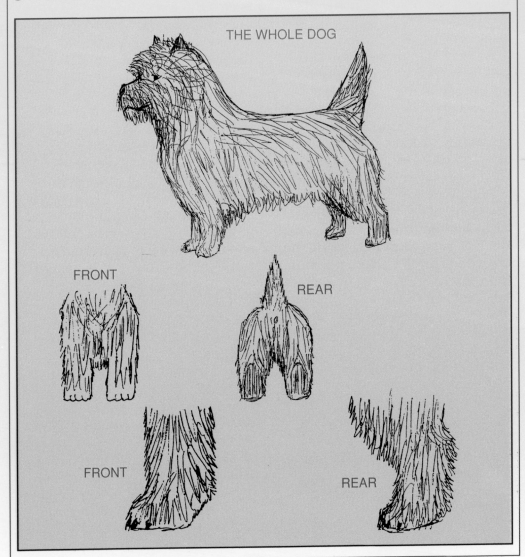

THE WHOLE DOG

FRONT

REAR

FRONT

REAR

straightened by using the posting method described in the section on show grooming. Usually you will find that the hair must be pulled very short on the inside of the leg just above the foot and left longer on the corresponding outside section of the leg. The same is true of hocks turned slightly inward or outward. Always picture the straight lines you want and by combing outward, pulling hair outside of the imaginary straight line, then combing back down to inspect the results, you can achieve the desired look. It is understood that any good judge will find these faults anyway, but you can still present the dog to its best advantage.

FEET

The most common problem is front feet that toe out too much. Keep the hair on the outer side of the foot very short and let the hair on the inner half grow a little longer. Again, picture the circle of a post meeting the ground and shape the foot with that picture in mind.

BODY TOO HIGH OR TOO LOW ON LEG

If your dog looks too high on leg, if his legs look too long for his body length, simply let the hair on his chest and belly grow longer. Conversely, if he is too low on leg, if his body looks too long for his height, use a stripping knife to shorten his chest and belly hair.

BODY TOO SHORT OR LONG

There is not much to do about the actual length of back of your dog, but you can increase the appearance of length by grooming the chest and the back of the thighs. If the coat on the front of the chest is combed to stick out somewhat forward and the coat on the back of the thighs just under the tail is combed to stick out back a bit, it will increase the look of body length. By doing the opposite, you can decrease the look of length. Neither is going to take an inch off or add one on, but it does help.

A longer-backed dog can also be made to look shorter when stacked by lifting the neck hair in front of the withers, then holding the head up and pulling it somewhat back while holding the tail slightly forward over the back. A shorter-backed dog's neck coat should be combed as close to his skin as possible. Hold his head up but not back and hold the tail upright or even a bit toward one o'clock. If he is a feisty little male, try to keep his hackles down. Raised hackles only shorten the back more.

IN CONCLUSION

It cannot be stressed enough that any dog with major or serious faults should not be exhibited nor bred. While minor faults can be groomed to look better, they should be bred out whenever possible. No dog is perfect, but only the best should be used in any breeding program.

AmCan. Ch. Foxairn Tinman, owned by Betty Hyslop, won Best of Breed at the 1994 Westminster Kennel Club dog show. Photo by Isabelle Francais.

Showing Your Cairn

by Chris Walkowicz

There are shows, and then there are shows.

All-breed shows and trials offer a bit of everything. Each entry is a purebred dog of a recognized breed, and at all-breed shows, there may be as many as 130 or more breeds entered. Trials are for obedience competition and may be held in conjunction with breed shows. Specialty shows are for one breed only, and national specialties are hosted by the national "parent" club, usually accompanied by a great deal of hoopla.

Field trials, tracking tests, hunting tests, herding tests and trials and other instinct tests are usually held outdoors and are often hosted separately. Instinct, agility and temperament tests are offered as added attractions more and more frequently at large all-breed and national shows.

At one time, all shows were benched with entries tied to their cubicles for spectators to observe. Now, benched shows have declined, and few are still in existence. Every dog lover should attend at least one of these benched events, either as a competitor or spectator. Some exhibitors decorate their benches and spread picnic lunches on grooming tables. Since the dogs are required to stay on their benches for several hours, it's a good opportunity for showing off the breeds, sharing knowledge, making contacts, observing other breeds, talking "dogs" and having a good time. At other exhibitions, it's usually "show and go."

Competitive events are showcases for the breeders' best. Sometimes it's more fun to observe, but true enthusiasts will tell you that when they aren't competing, they feel the itch.

As with any other passion, showing is a progressive disease. It starts slowly with a yen to have the dog behave and show well, to be in the placings, to obtain a leg or a point. Once that goal is attained, excitement mounts and the drive is on to reach the top in our field: Championship, a Best of Breed, a Group I, a Best in Show, Top-winning Dog; a High in Trial, a 200 score, an OTCh, Super Dog at the Gaines Classic; a field or herding trial placement, an instinct Championship, National Gun Dog Champion.

DOG SHOW MANIA

Most first-time buyers have no interest in showing. Oftimes the show bug bites the unsuspecting shortly after joining a training class. Following the initial exposure, the future show addict weakens and the "disease" settles in for a long-term stay and occasionally is terminal.

As the weeks proceed, we note how smart and/or beautiful our dog is compared to the others in the class. When a notice is passed about a nearby match, we decide to enter just for the fun of it. That's why it's called a fun match.

People go and have a good time, and so do the dogs. The atmosphere is relaxed, other

AmCan. Ch. Terriwood's Lasting Legacy, a Cairn Terrier Club of Canada Best of Breed winner. Owners, Tom and Karin Godwin. Photo by Animal World Studio.

novice exhibitors and untrained pups are entered, and although winning makes the day even more fun, competition is not intense. Win or lose, those who have succumbed to the bug soon find another match or two and then begin thinking about shows.

Time marches on, and so do we . . . to the beat of a different drummer. Weekends are consumed by showing and doggy interests: conformation, obedience, field trials and instinct tests. Weeknights we attend club meetings to plan these events. Our wardrobe consists of tweeds, mohairs, washable suits, all with running shoes to match and with pockets for bait.

The family vehicle has grown from a sedan to a station wagon or van, and it bears a bumper sticker saying, "I'd rather be at a dog show." Realtors start calling about the five acres for sale just outside of town.

By this point, the enthusiast is eyeing another dog or three and planning the kennel building with indoor/ outdoor runs.

Often our first dog does not take the pro world by its ear, and we decide that ol' Phydeaux can enjoy life by the fireside while we set forth to search for the Wonder Pup that stirs the judges' blood.

Depending on our experience

and knowledge, we demand *top show quality* and qualify this with specifics: showmanship, natural instinct, a gorgeous head, superior movement, intelligence, and so on.

We know what we want—perfection. The trick is obtaining or breeding that ideal . . . or even coming close to it. That's what showing is all about: the quest for the ideal. To

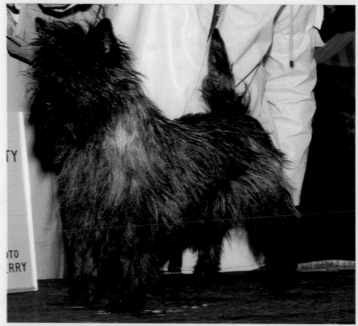

Ch. Killarney's Image of Wildwood owned by Mr. and Mrs. Robert B. Williams.

reach that unreachable star. It's not exactly tilting at windmills, because some come close—close enough to touch the star's tip, to be thrilled by its warmth. But perfection has not yet been attained. No dog scores 200 every time it walks into the obedience ring, and never has one remained unbeaten for its career in the breed ring.

CLUBS

Joining a club is probably the best way to learn, advance and eventually help others attain their goals. Almost anywhere there are dogs, there is a dog club. More than 3,000 dog clubs exist, and these clubs host approximately 10,000 AKC-sanctioned events annually.

Clubs bring together people interested in a common cause, in this case, their dogs. Whether we want to attain a conformation or obedience title, to breed better animals or simply to enjoy our canine companion, we can do it in the company of others who love dogs.

It's encouraging to have friends cheer us on in our attempts. Tailgate parties are more fun when friends are along, and when several club members attend a show, there's usually someone who has cause to celebrate.

Most clubs hold annual shows, matches and other doggy events such as instinct tests, seminars, demonstrations and training classes. A list of breeders within the club is made available to

Ch. Tagalong of Wildwood out of Ch. Cairnwood's Quince x Ch. Milbryan Killarney O'Carimar. She is a specialty winner and the dam of several champions. Owners, Mr. and Mrs. Robert B. Williams.

can have company who doesn't care about dog hair in the coffee and who comes to visit wearing jeans already marked with paw prints.

Club membership is caravaning to shows, helping to tow another member out of a mud-sucking field or jump-starting a battery on a sub-zero day. Members care about each other and about their dogs.

those searching for puppies or studs.

Most important, a club consists of members. Members who hold our hand when our pal is in surgery, who bring the bubbly when our dog finishes and who offer advice and company during a whelping.

It's having friends who help us through the hard times or who hold an extra dog at ringside. No matter what happens, someone has already walked in our shoes. When we come in fifth out of five, have a pup going through the teenage ganglies or own a bitch who has trouble conceiving, someone can usually console us and either offer advice or supply the name of someone who can. Being a club member means we

TRAINING

Training classes are offered through these organizations and by experienced individuals. Although it's possible to train a dog without attending a class, it's difficult to test an animal's abilities without distractions. With other dogs and people around, our dog may find them more interesting than our commands. But dogs have to learn to behave under any circumstance. Many an owner claims, "I can't understand it. He does it all fine at home."

A class instructor knows how to solve a problem when teams are at a stalemate in an exercise and can correct us when we're doing something wrong to lead the dog astray. Besides, group training is sure more fun than doing it by ourselves.

Training is valuable for all dogs and all owners, not just those who are going into competition. Probably 80 percent of all people who register for a training class simply want a well-behaved companion. The all-important bonding is intensified when dog and master learn to work together and develop respect for one another.

Training doesn't stop with class, however. It continues at home, through practicing the stack, the stay, moving on leash, and through bringing out the best in our dogs by conditioning them.

CONDITIONING

Making sure our dog is in prime condition at all times includes training, exercising, grooming, instilling confidence and seeking veterinary care. Although it's best to begin exposing the dog to various situations by eight weeks, it can be accomplished at older ages if a newcomer to the sport decides to jump in.

Professional breeders begin handling their pups at birth, gently touching, caressing and talking to them. As the pups grow, they are exposed to household noise and activity. No one goes through life tiptoeing about. Dropped pots and slammed doors are a part of our lives and our dogs'.

Nail clipping begins, as a necessity, at one week of age or the dam pays the penalty with painful scratches on her sensitive breasts. Breeders weigh each individual, offering tiny tidbits and loving caresses. Setting pups on tables and gently brushing them is good practice for all dogs, show or pet, and should begin in small doses at five or six weeks. Pups should learn to walk on various footing—lawns, carpets

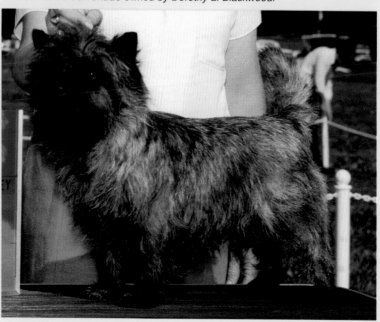

Ch. Cairnhoe Carronade owned by Dorothy L. Blackwood.

and linoleum.

When the litter is about six weeks old, leash training can begin with pups following the dam or walking at will with the owner following them. After a few days of this, the owner can start changing directions, clucking and talking to the pup, encouraging it to follow.

Games such as hide and seek teach the puppies that owners do return, and a little later encourage the dogs to use their noses to find people and objects. Chasing a ball

sanctioned matches and shows are open to dogs at least six months of age. Even if the puppy isn't ready for serious competition, matches make excellent socialization opportunities. The most important thing for the dog—and us—is to have a good time.

More serious training, accompanied by firm commands and gentle corrections, can begin as soon as puppies begin challenging authority, much like the human toddler. This occurs at various times, according to the individual. Some puppies are born angels. Most aren't!

Exercise at will is important from the beginning. Most dogs know when they've had enough. Road working to condition muscles or programmed jumping should not be undertaken until the dog is past puberty to forestall injuries to pliable growing bones.

Ch. Cairnhouse Wildstar with Junior Showmanship handler Chris Howse winning first place under Beryl Gould.

and returning it for more tosses introduces the retrieve.

As soon as the first vaccination is given, acclimation to crates and traveling can begin, heading for parks, training classes and other fun places, not just the vet clinic. Fun matches offer classes for two-month-old puppies, and

CONFORMATION

Exhibitors who like conformation showing champion the cause with gusto. It's more than just a beauty contest, enthusiasts claim. It's an attempt to breed the dog closest to the standard, improving on each generation. It's being instrumental in the creation of a dog who causes a sensation, a murmur in the crowd. The dog who always draws the spectators and surreptitious glances from the judges in the adjoining rings.

It's handling that dog to countless Best of Breed (BOB), Group and Best in Show (BIS) wins, smashing records and setting new ones. And moving around the yard with a youngster who never sets a foot down wrong and knowing . . . just knowing . . . that this

Shin Pond Ashbey owned by Laura DeVincent.

is the one that will take you all the way, close enough to snag that star.

We soon learn the jargon and doggy etiquette. Fifteen points make a Champion; nine of these points may be obtained in minor (one or two-point) competition. Two majors (three to five points) are required, and at least three judges must have found the dog worthy of receiving points.

Majors are do-or-die occasions. Because majors are almost as scarce as tickets to the World Series and just about as difficult to win, one does not cause that major to break by withdrawing a dog unless one has a death wish.

But all of this starts with a first training class, where the handler and the pup learn to walk, and then run, without tripping over each other. Here the trainer teaches the handlers to bring out the best in their dogs and to look graceful while doing so. Some of us never attain this ability and hire a professional to do the job.

Handlers are convenient. Showing is their job, and they don't have bosses grumbling when they take time off work to attend events. Because they are able to travel and participate in more shows, their dogs win more frequently. Because their dogs win more frequently, they attain more clients. And compete more often, and win more often. And on and on and on.

Breeders often have other

Ch. Shin Pond Dreyfus owned by Laura DeVincent.

our dog. Most handlers specialize within a group or type. For instance, one person may handle all terriers, but nothing else. Another concentrates on "coaty" dogs, such as the Poodle, Bichon Frise and Pomeranian.

Find out who wins consistently at shows and ask other owners for advice. Observe, also, the handler's treatment of her dogs. Does she truly like dogs? Do she and her dogs look like a team when competing? Or is this only a way to earn extra money on weekends?

Ask to watch the grooming session. Is he thorough, yet gentle? Do his charges like him? Notice whether he is firm or rough in his methods. Cleanliness of facilities and exercise areas counts too.

Owners should be compatible with their dogs' handlers, and so should the animals. If there is a personality clash, someone's going to lose. Most times, it's the dog.

Ascertain the fees before making any verbal or written agreement to hire someone. A few professionals charge a higher fee per show, but cover expenses themselves. Most charge expenses

commitments besides jobs. There are spouses, "What! You're going another weekend?" Children, "But, Dad, I wanna go to the beach." And whelping demands, "So you want me to cross my hocks until you come back, or what?"

Because handling is their career, pros have the experience and finesse amateurs often lack. When a person spends 40 hours a week doing something, he or she is usually more competent than those of us who eke out an hour or two of our spare time.

Occasionally, an owner doesn't attend any of the shows but sends the dog off with a professional until the Championship or honors sought are attained. Once the decision is made to hire a pro, we must decide who is the best for in addition to their fee.

You may be able to share expenses if the handler has several other clients, but that usually means sharing time as well. Ask what happens when she has a conflict in another ring. Some handlers have assistants or work out reciprocal agreements with other pros.

Discuss all possibilities in advance: veterinary care, bonuses for special wins, splitting of cash awards, length of commitment, and so on. Even if you send your dog with the handler for a period of time, she should call regularly to let you know how he's doing and to work out further details. That's the meaning of—and the reason for—a professional.

Everyone has different methods of obtaining goals. With some, the game is incomplete unless they themselves breed, train and exhibit their dogs. Others are content with buying a superstar and cheering from the sidelines. Still others fall somewhere in between. Whatever the route, the final destination is the same, to own a dog that excites the senses—and the judge.

For many exhibitors, the challenge lies at specialty shows. Winning under a judge who has a depth of knowledge about—and perhaps has bred, owned and/or exhibited—this particular breed is a coup, particularly when the win is over a large number of other quality entries. Gaining the nod at a national specialty show is especially gratifying. There will

Ch. Cairmar Courtesan, a Best in Show winner, owned by Betty Marcum.

Ch. Cairmar Winston O'Lincairn, owned by Betty Marcum. Photo by Missy Yuhl.

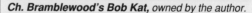

Ch. Bramblewood's Bob Kat, owned by the author.

The Red Knight of Misty Moor, CDX, Can. CD. Photo by Dawn Burdick.

At discovering the yet untapped intelligence of our dogs, we yearn to find out just how good they really are.

For many owners, the goal is to gain titles (Companion Dog, CD; Companion Dog Excellent, CDX; Utility Dog, UD; Utility Dog Excellent, UDX) which proclaim their pets' ability and their own prowess in training. Three passes (or legs) under three judges, and that's enough.

But a few hone the competitive edge, going for an Obedience Trial Championship (OTCh), as well as top wins in individual breeds and in all-breeds. To win an OTCh, the dog must garner 100 points from winning first or second placings in Open and Utility Classes against all breeds, including those who already have their OTCh. Capturing High in Trial (HIT), whether at an all-breed, specialty or national show, is a coup that all serious competitors seek.

Special trials such as the Windsor Classic, the Gaines Regionals and Classic—which is considered the Super Bowl of the obedience world—attract the best working teams in the country. Amazing precision does not remove the obvious pleasure of the dog to be working with his

always be a thrill at being chosen the best among one's peers.

Most people compete at all-breed shows frequently, however, possibly because there are more of these events than specialties. Here the excitement mounts as each hurdle is met and overcome: the class win, Winners, Breed, Group and ultimately BIS. These achievements feed the progressive urge to conquer.

OBEDIENCE

Many owners sign up for a training class, hoping the results will give them a well-behaved pet.

best friend.

All of this brings the bonus of a good companion, one with enough manners to keep his nose out of the guests' cocktail glass and who waits politely for his own potato chip without too much drooling or too many mournful looks.

TRACKING

When it comes to tracking, our dogs always beat us by a nose. Canines have 40 times more olfactory sensory cells than humans do, and that's why they have such busy noses. Why not put to good use all that business of tracing down every crumb on the floor and sniffing at each other and visitors in embarrassing places?

Tracking, unlike the other obedience titles, can be earned at any time, before the CD, after the UDX or anywhere in between.

A dog's been using his nose since birth when he followed it to his mother's table setting. Allowing the dog to do what comes naturally is not always easy for owners, however, because we're used to running the show. Training to track often consists of teaching the handler to "lay off" and to take directions from the dog, as well as steering the dog's nose in the right direction and on command.

The second hardest thing

Ch. Cairmar's Sparkling Star, Can. CD, owned by Susan Ensley. Who says Cairns don't do obedience?

about tracking is forgetting about creature comforts. Tracks are laid in the rain, the cold and the heat, as well as on beautiful, balmy days. They're laid in muck and frost and amongst ragweed tickling our noses, as well as in lovely, grassy pastures. Over hill and dale in addition to flat surfaces. You get the picture—

The broad jump is no "hurdle" for **Toby**. Owner, Cindy Eli.

training must also be performed under such conditions so that the dog tracks during any trick of Mother Nature. Not only that, early morning is the best time to train while the dew is still on the roses. . . and the ground.

If you and your dog hold up to snuff and enjoy the great outdoors, then there's the TDX (Tracking Dog Excellent).

CANINE CITIZENSHIP

In an effort to promote responsible dog ownership and good canine members of society, the AKC approved the Canine Good Citizen Tests in 1989. We have long since passed the time when dogs were allowed to roam at will—creating destruction, havoc and more puppies or alternatively being fed by the butcher, the baker and the candlemaker with benign good will. Today's dog must learn to adapt to modern, crowded society.

Dogs perform the tests on leash and are graded either pass or fail. The evaluators consider the following:

1. Does this dog's behavior make him the kind of dog which they would like to own?

2. Would this dog be safe with children?

3. Would this dog be welcome as their neighbor?

4. Does this dog make his owner happy—without making others unhappy?

There are ten tests. The dog must:

1. Be clean, groomed, healthy, and allow touching and brushing by the evaluator.

2. Accept a stranger's approach.

3. Walk on a loose lead under control—as though out on a walk.

4. Walk through a crowd.

5. Sit for an exam while a stranger pets him.

6. Sit and down on command.

7. Stay in position. Additionally, the entry is judged on its reaction to:

8. Another dog.

9. Distractions such as loud noises, sudden appearance of a person or a person with an object such as a bicycle.

10. Being left alone for five minutes.

When it comes to tracking, our Cairns beat us by a nose! Photo by Robert Smith.

Cairn Terrier competing in obedience. Photo by Karen Taylor.

INSTINCT TESTING

During the 1980s, the American Kennel Club encouraged getting back to the basics training with instinct tests. Their hunting tests began in 1985 and have been enormously successful, growing faster than anyone expected.

In 1990, AKC approved herding tests as a sanctioned sport. National clubs encourage natural instincts by sponsoring water tests for Newfs, tunnel tests for terriers, lure coursing for sighthounds, coaching trials for Dalmatians, weight pulling and carting for working dogs, and sledding for Nordic breeds. The only test for toy breeds at present is a daily one for all dogs— companions for their owners.

All of these instinct tests are pass or fail. Either the dog does it . . . or he doesn't. This format is great for the pet owner who simply wants to see if his dog can do what he was supposed to do 100 or more years ago when the breed was first developed. The tests are also a way for the show exhibitor to prove that, yes, his dog can do more than be pretty. Yes, he can work like he was meant to.

Hunting tests are divided into Junior, Senior and Master stakes with different formats for retrievers, pointing dogs and flushing spaniels. Basic herding test classes are divided into Preliminary and Principal. When the dog has passed both, he receives an HT (Herding Tested). The more complicated Pretrial Test shows more advanced training and a passing dog receives a PT (Pretrial Tested).

When a dog has never before been trained or exposed to his erstwhile duties, it's amazing and exciting for owners to watch a dog "turn on." As the dog's attention is caught, his posture changes to one of alertness. Eyes become intense and muscles twitch in readiness.

These tests are also good news for the person who is non-competitive or has limited time or budget to spend on doggy activities. Further information on these events may be obtained from the American Kennel Club, Performance Events Dept., 51 Madison Avenue, New York, NY 10010, and through books written on these particular subjects.

Yes, a dog can be attractive and conform to the standard and can still work. Maybe next, truffle hunting trials for Poodles.

AGILITY

Agility is almost more fun than work, and it's certainly fun for those watching it. Although a few people are beginning to take it seriously, most entries simply want to see if their dog can and will conquer the obstacles.

Originating in the United Kingdom in 1977, agility has begun popping up at more and more American shows as well. The object is for the dog to take on each obstacle as quickly as possible and without making a mistake. These include jumps, a

Although Cairns aren't seen at agility trials too regularly, when they are it's a real crowd pleaser. This Cairn is clearing the bar jump. Photo by Karen Taylor.

scaling wall, a rigid tunnel, a collapsible tunnel, a hoop, seesaw, wall, water jump and almost any other barrier a club can invent. There are also a table and a pause box, where the dog must stand on top for five seconds.

The best time and performance wins. Relay teams increase the challenge and fun. Clubs may offer courses for large dogs and for small dogs. Agility is held as a non-regular obedience class under AKC rules.

AKC EARTHDOG TESTS

Cairns and their owners will really dig the newest in AKC terrier events: Earthdog Tests! The Cairn, along with his fellow low-legged terriers and the ubiquitous Dachshund, can now add new letters to his name. Namely, JE, SE and ME. These new titles, effective July 1994,

indicate that the dog has passed the required tests for Junior Earthdog, Senior Earthdog, and finally Master Earthdog. After completing the Introductory Test, where the terrier has to reach its quarry within two minutes and "work" it for 30 seconds, he qualifies for entry to the first tests for the JE. To "work" its quarry, the terrier must bark, growl, lunge, and bite at its cornered rat. Although terrier quarry typically includes badgers, foxes, and otters, AKC doesn't feel these are practical; laboratory rats will have to do until a mechanical decoy is designed. As the dog passes to the next level of competition, different tunnels, underground obstacles, false dens, a second dog, etc., are introduced.

There is no doubt that Earthdog Tests will be every Cairn's favorite AKC event—a lot more fun than posing for a liver snap!

Prevention and Cure = A Healthy Life

by Chris Walkowicz

Every owner hopes that his dog will live a long healthy life. Nowadays, this desire is enhanced through careful selection of puppies and breeding animals, modern technology and veterinary care and the family's care and concern—all of which aid in prevention and cure.

Dogs today are so much more fortunate than their ancestors. Regulations which were originally passed to protect property, livestock and humans actually ensure a dog's safety as well. Licenses and the accompanying taxes provide shelters for lost or abandoned animals, and a tag may prove to be a lifeline to home. Because leashes and confinement are now required by law, fewer families allow Rover to rove and have his life ended by a bullet or highway traffic.

Ch. Gayla Cairns Supercharge owned by Carolyn Myers.

Many diseases commonly fatal in the early to mid-1900s are now prevented through inoculation. An old-time exhibitor understood that if he took his dog to enough shows, the animal would contract distemper sooner or later. It was common to lose entire litters to the dread disease, which plagued canines for hundreds of years. Now, thanks to nearly universal vaccination,

Four-month-old Cairn puppies ready for the world!

most breeders have never even seen a case.

As recently as 1978, parvovirus swept the canine world, decimating kennels. As with all diseases, it was the very young and the very elderly dogs that succumbed in great numbers. Thanks to modern research laboratories and the pharmaceutical companies, this time within two years a preventative vaccine was available.

GENERAL MEDICAL CARE

Before a puppy is sold, he should have received at least one full set of inoculations, protecting him from distemper, hepatitis

199

*Open wide! This is **Ch. Tosaig Dawn's Delight** owned by John and Nancy Cassel.*

and rabies.

Before the puppy goes to his new home, he should be examined by a veterinarian and pronounced healthy and free of major congenital defects. Most bite, eyelid, testiculate, cardial and esophagael problems can be detected before eight weeks, as can luxated patellas and open fontanels. From that point on, it's up to the new owners to continue examinations and veterinary care to keep him healthy. Routine health care, of course, includes yearly vaccinations and heartworm checks, followed by administration of the preventative.

(adenovirus), leptospirosis, parainfluenza and parvo. Many breeders vaccinate against corona virus and bordatella as well. Among the puppy's stack of official papers that are turned over to the expectant parents should be a list noting the ages when additional shots will be needed. Although the schedule varies from breeder to breeder, or one veterinarian to another, the following is an example: six weeks—combination DA2PP & Cv; nine weeks—parvo; 12 weeks—combination; 16 weeks—parvo

DENTAL CARE

Dogs can't be fitted with dentures, so it's up to us to assure that their teeth last them as long as possible. Dry foods or a mixture of canned and dry help the teeth and gums remain healthy. Feeding only moist or canned dog food can allow food to stick around the gumline, causing gums to become inflamed or teeth to decay. Even with a diet of dry food, tartar (plaque) can accumulate.

Cleaning our dog's teeth with a veterinary dentifrice, or a mixture of baking soda and water, is suggested and should be done at least once a week. The act of rubbing with a toothbrush and/or cleaning plaque with a dental tool is more important than the product used.

In this area, as well as others, never substitute your own products for those specifically made for animals without asking a veterinarian. Human toothpaste or shampoos, for example, can actually be detrimental to our pets' care.

PARASITES

Taking stool samples to the vet should be part of the annual examination or when observing symptoms such as diarrhea, bloody stools or worm segments. Dogs, especially puppies, may vomit and lose weight when infested with parasites. Hookworms, roundworms, tapeworms, whipworms, coccidia and giardia are common. They can be eradicated with the proper medication but could be dangerous if left untreated. An over-the-counter drug may not be the right one for the particular parasite which your dog is harboring.

FLEAS

Bugs bug us and our pets. Fleas cause itching and carry tapeworm eggs. The resultant scratching can irritate the skin so that rashes and hot spots develop.

Dogs lose hair, scratch and chew at themselves and are miserable. In attempting to exterminate the pests, owners tear their hair, scratch their heads, chew their nails and are also miserable. Better to prevent than to cure, but for everyone's sanity, once the invasion has occurred, the sooner

Washing your Cairn with a flea and tick shampoo will help to eradicate these pests. Photo courtesy of Hagen.

the evacuation, the better.

Talk to your veterinarian about the proper products to use, then arrange a regular reconnaissance to prevent a losing battle with fleas. During the warm months of the year, many people spray or powder animals (including other pets who may pass fleas to your dogs) once a week and premises (house and lawn) once a month. In between, owners keep up flea surveillance. At the slightest

Ch. Ohioville Rooster owned by Eleanor Buesing.

sleeping quarters. It doesn't do any good to treat the animal without debugging the environment or vice-versa. One flea who escapes will happily reinfest all over again. If the infestation is heavy, it may be necessary to fog your house and to repeat the procedure a few weeks later. All animals must be removed from the premises for the period of time specified on the fogger can.

In addition to the regular regime, many owners spray before walking dogs in areas where they are likely to pick them up, e.g., woods, pastures, training and show grounds. Most flea pesticides also kill ticks, and daily grooming sessions should include running your fingers through the dog's coat to find engorged ticks. Natural, non-insecticidal products can safely be used on a daily basis in the on-going war on fleas.

scratch, they look for telltale evidence—skittering teeny bugs or flea dirt, which looks like a sprinkling of pepper. It's usually easiest to see the freeloaders on the less hairy groin, belly or just above the root of the tail.

Among the products used to combat flea pests are dips, collars, powders, sprays, tags and internals—drops or pills. Instructions should be followed implicitly not only for best results, but because some of these products contain ingredients which may cause problems themselves if used carelessly.

If the critters are found, shampoo or dip all dogs (cats, too, with a product labeled safe for them), and spray living and

LYME DISEASE

One species of tick, *Ixodes scapularis,* the tiny deer tick, is one of the culprits which transmit the germ that causes Lyme disease to humans and animals. Deer ticks are found on mammals and birds, as well as in grasses, trees and shrubs. They are rarely visible because they are so small (as minute as the dot above an i), but the damage they can cause is magnified many times their size.

Lyme disease can damage the joints, kidneys, heart, brain and immune system in canines and humans. Symptoms can include a rash, fever, lameness, fatigue, nausea, aching body and personality change among others. Left untreated, the disease can lead to arthritis, deafness, blindness, miscarriages and birth defects, heart disease and paralysis. It may prove to be fatal.

People should cover themselves with protective clothing while outdoors to prevent bites. Repellents are helpful for both dogs and humans. Examine the body after excursions and see a doctor if symptoms appear.

SKIN DISORDERS

Dogs, just like people, can suffer from allergies. While people most often have respiratory symptoms, dogs usually exhibit their allergies through itching, scratching, chewing or licking their irritated skin. These irritations often lead to angry, weeping "hot" spots.

Allergies are easy to detect but difficult to treat. Medications and topical substances can be useful, in addition to avoidance of the irritant, if possible.

CERF/OFA/VWD CERTIFICATION

Good breeders want to produce healthy, sound animals. The best

Always run your fingers through your Cairn's coat to check for fleas and engorged ticks after he has been outside. **Renart's Maggie MacPhee** *is enjoying a lovely day outdoors. Photo by Patricia Holmes.*

way to do this is to start with healthy, normal animals judged to be free of hereditary conditions which can cause lameness, blindness and other disorders.

In the early years of dog shows, when symptoms of disease appeared, owners asked the opinion of experienced local breeders and veterinarians. As time went on, more specifics were learned about these various diseases and their heritability. Veterinarians took x-rays, performed blood tests and diagnosed symptoms. Now we are fortunate to have experts in various areas. Due to their specialized training and the numbers of cases these experts see, they are more likely to be accurate. Some have formed organizations which register clear animals and certify dogs free of hereditary disease.

Probably the first organization of its type, the Orthopedic Foundation for Animals (OFA) certifies dogs free of hip dysplasia upon clearance of an x-ray by three board-certified radiologists. Dogs must be two years old for lifetime certification. The OFA also reads and gives opinions of radiographs with evidence of other heritable bone disorders such as craniomandibular osteopathy (CMO), osteochondritis dissecans (OCD), ununited anchoneal process, Legg-Perthes disease and fragmented chronoid process. The organization's address is OFA, 2300 Nifong Blvd., Columbia, MO 65201.

Eye problems can be detected by veterinary opthalmologists available at teaching hospitals, private specialty practices (in larger cities) and at eye-screening clinics hosted by kennel clubs. These specialists examine for cataracts, entropion, pannus, retinal dysplasia, luxated lens, progressive retinal atrophy (PRA), central progressive retinal

Topical solutions can help to soothe and heal your dog's wounds and other skin irritations. Photo courtesy of Hagen.

atrophy, Collie eye anomaly and other hereditary eye conditions. The Canine Eye Registration Foundation (CERF) may be contacted at CERF Veterinary Medicine Data Program, South Campus Courts, Bldg. C., Purdue University, West Lafayette, IN 47907. The age of the dog at first testing depends a great deal on the breed and the specific area of concern. A few diseases are apparent in puppyhood. CERF

Ch. Copperglen Fame N' Fortune, a C.T.C.A. national specialty winner bred and owned by Chuck and Carol Ackerson.

requires annual examination for certification of freedom from some diseases.

Von Willebrand's disease (vWD) is a bleeding disorder, similar to hemophilia. Clinical signs include lameness, aching joints, bloody stools, chronic bloody ear infections or a failure of the blood to clot. A blood test measures for adequate concentration of a specific clotting factor. Although it may be conducted in puppies as young as seven weeks, it should not be done within one month of vaccination; therefore, most are five or six months old. If a dog is in heat, has just whelped a litter or has been on antibiotics, the test should also be postponed for one month. Other disorders that are limited to just one or two breeds also have specific tests. Blood samples can be sent by your veterinarian to Dr. Jean Dodds, Veterinary Hematology Laboratory, Wadsworth Center for Laboratories and Research, NY State Dept. of Health, PO Box 509, Albany, NY 12201-0509.

Before you breed, determine whether or not your dog is free of these and other hereditary diseases. Although the tests involve some cost, they are not as expensive as attempting to replace faulty pups. And they are certainly much less costly than a broken heart or a damaged reputation.

BONE DISEASE

Many canine bone diseases have gained nicknames—albeit not affectionate—due to the unwieldy medical terminology. For instance, canine cervical vertebral malformation/malarticulation syndrome is referred to as "wobbler" syndrome; panosteitis is shortened to pano; and canine hip dysplasia is often simply called CHD. The first symptom is usually a limp. Diagnosis is made through a radiograph of the affected area.

Craniomandibular osteopathy (CMO) affects the growth of bone in the lower jaw, causing severe pain. Spondylosis is the technical name for spinal arthritis.

Hip dysplasia is a poor fit of the hip joint into the socket, which causes erosion. Wobbler syndrome affects the neck vertebrae, causing weakness in the hindquarters and eventually the forequarters. Osteochondrosis dissecans (OCD)

Ch. Ohioville Hooper cooling off in a mountain spring. Owner, Eleanor Buesing.

A couple of clever Cairns catching up on some reading. Owner, Betty Marcum.

affects joints, most often the shoulder, elbow or stifle. Ununited anchoneal process, commonly referred to as elbow dysplasia, is a failure of the growth line to close, thereby creating a loose piece in the joint. Kneecaps which pop out of the proper position are diagnosed as luxating patellas. Legg-Perthes, most often seen in small breeds, is a collapsing of the hip joint. They all result in the same thing: pain, lameness and, left untreated, arthritis.

The exception is pano, which is a temporary affliction causing discomfort during youth. Pano may be visible on x-rays, showing up as a cloudiness in the bone marrow in the long bones, particularly in fast-growing breeds.

EYES

Entropion is a condition in which the eyelid rolls inward. Eyelashes rub and irritate the

Ch. Cairnbrae's Hint of Gold owned by Ann F. Kerr. Photo by Robert Tomarantz.

cornea. In ectropion, the lower eyelid sags outward, allowing dirt to catch in the exposed sensitive area and irritate the eye. In addition, extra eyelashes grow inside the lid which rub the surface of the eye and cause tearing. Either can be treated topically or, if severe, surgically.

ORGANIC DISEASE

Heart disease affects canines much as it does humans. A dog suffering from a problem involving the heart may exhibit weakness, fainting, difficulty breathing, a persistent cough, loss of appetite, abdominal swelling due to fluid retention, exhaustion following normal exercise, or even heart failure and sudden death. Upon examination, an abnormal heart rhythm or sound or electrical potential might be detected, or changes in speed or strength noticed.

Treatment includes first stabilizing any underlying condition, followed by medications, low-sodium diet, exercise restriction and, possibly, surgery.

Chronic renal disease may first show up in vague symptoms—

lethargy, diarrhea, anemia, weight loss and lack of appetite—as well as increased thirst and urination. Kidney disease is more common among geriatric canines. It may be compensated to some extent through diet. Diagnosis is most often made through blood and urine tests.

owners, particularly of large breeds, know there is no time to waste whether it's the middle of the night, a holiday or vacation time. It is urgent to reach a veterinarian who can treat the shock, followed by surgery to reposition the twisted organs. During surgery, the veterinarian

GASTRIC TORSION

Because a dog's stomach hangs like a hammock, the ends are effectively shut off if it flips over. Nothing can enter or exit. The normal bacterial activity in the stomach causes gas to build with no release through vomiting or defecating. The gas expands and, just like a balloon filled with helium, the stomach bulges and bloats.

It's physical torture for the dog and mental anguish for the owner who sees his dog moaning in agony and retching in a futile attempt to relieve the pressure.

With the veins and arteries to the stomach and spleen also closed off, shock sets in which can be rapidly fatal. Torsion—medically termed gastric dilatation and volvulus (GDV)—is an emergency. Experienced

Life's a beach for this trio of Cairn Terriers. Owner, Patricia Holmes.

may tack the stomach to the abdominal wall to prevent recurrence.

AUTO-IMMUNE DISEASES

Auto-immune disease, like cancer, is an umbrella term that includes many diseases of similar origin but showing different symptoms. Literally, the body's immune system views one of its own organs or tissues as foreign and launches an attack on it. Symptoms depend on which system is the target.

For instance, hypothyroidism symptoms can include lethargy, musty odor, temperament change, decreased fertility or unexplained weight gain, in addition to the more suggestive thin dry hair, scaliness of the skin, and thickness and darkening of the skin. Testing for hypothyroidism (which can be from causes other than auto-immune disease) may be conducted as early as eight to twelve months, using the complete blood count, blood chemistry, thyroid T4, T3 and free T4 tests.

Rheumatoid arthritis is a result of an auto-immune reaction to the joint surfaces. The resulting inflammation and swelling causes painful deformed joints. If the red blood cells are perceived as foreign invaders and destroyed, the rapid onset anemia (called auto-immune hemolytic anemia) can cause collapse and death if diagnosis and treatment are not quickly initiated. Often an auto-immune reaction in an organ causes destruction of that organ with subsequent loss of function. Auto-immune disease of the adrenal gland leads to hypoadrenocortissism (Addison's disease.)

The same reaction in the thyroid gland soon has the dog exhibiting symptoms of hypothyroidism. Auto-immune diseases of the skin are called pemphigus, while those of connective tissue are termed lupus. Many other varieties exist, and each requires specialized testing and biopsy. Most respond to treatment once a diagnosis is made.

EPILEPSY

Probably because of the feeling of helplessness, one of the most frightening situations a dog owner can face is watching a beloved dog suffer seizures. As in people, epilepsy is a neurological condition which may be controlled by anticonvulsant drugs. Many breeds of dogs have a hereditary form

Cairnkeep Fiery Teegan and *Ch. Cairnkeep Call Me Camron.*
Photo by Dawn Burdick.

of epilepsy usually with an adult onset.

The University of Pennsylvania Canine Epilepsy Service has conducted studies of drugs and dosages, their efficacy and long-term side effects, to assist veterinarians in prescribing anticonvulsants.

ALTERNATIVE TECHNIQUES

During the 1970s and '80s, acupuncture, chiropractic and holistic medicine became part of the canine health picture. Veterinarians who have received special training in these fields now practice their techniques on patients who do not respond to or cannot take previously prescribed medical treatments. Patients have responded favorably to these methods, especially when done in conjunction with medical supervision. Certainly, when it comes to a much-loved animal, the most recent up-to-date techniques should be tried before resorting to euthanasia.

Owners should be aware, however, that practitioners must have a veterinary degree to practice on animals and that the holistic, chiropractic and

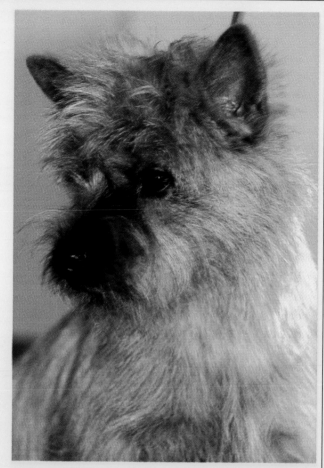

For all of the love and devotion your Cairn has afforded you, proper care can never be too costly. Photo by Patricia Holmes.

acupunctural treatment should not take the place of standard veterinary medicine, but enhance it.

GERIATRICS

As dogs age, problems are more likely to occur, just as they do in their human counterparts. It is even more important to examine your dogs, noting every "normal" lump and sag, so that if a new one occurs you are aware. Owners should make appointments for

Renart's Maggie MacPhee sitting on top of the world. Photo by Pat Holmes.

Although our dogs will never live long enough to satisfy us, we can extend their lives through our precautions, specialized nutrition, exercise and routine veterinary care.

EMERGENCIES

The get-your-vet-on-the-phone-drive-there-as-quickly-as-is-safe emergency situations are few, thankfully. But they do occur, and that's why all owners should be aware of symptoms. Veterinarian numbers for day and night calls should be posted prominently near the phone.

Occasions that are well worth a middle-of-the-night payment are: shock, anoxia (choking), dystocia (labor and whelping complications), hemorrhage, gastric torsion, electric shock, large wounds, compound fractures and heat stroke. In addition, neurological symptoms such as paralysis, convulsions and unconsciousness indicate an emergency. If your dog has ingested poison, been severely burned or hit by a car, for instance, call an emergency number for help.

veterinary check-ups at least once a year.

Elderly canines suffer the same infirmities as we do when we age. Deafness, arthritis, cancers, organ disease and loss of vision are common. Symptoms such as a cough, bloating, weight loss, increased water consumption and a dry thin coat are warning signs to seek medical attention. Many aging patients can be made comfortable and sustain a quality life.

EUTHANASIA

Most owners dread facing the decision of euthanizing a pet. But as hard as it is to make that decision and drive a beloved animal on his final journey, it is more difficult to watch a dog who has lost all quality of life struggle through a day-to-day fog of pain. Of course, it's also more stressful for the animal, and don't we love him enough to spare him that trauma? Certainly, eyes that plead "Help me" deserve a humane response.

Euthanasia is a fact that most breeders and pet owners must eventually face if they do not wish their animals to suffer. Ask your veterinarian to administer a non-lethal anesthetic or tranquilizer, literally putting the dog to sleep while you hold your pet and caress him gently. The dog will drift off to sleep peacefully and without fear, no longer suffering. At that point, the veterinarian injects a lethal overdose of anesthesia which instantly stops the heart. Death truly comes as a servant in peace; euthanasia is a kind, quiet death.

Arrangements should be made for the disposition of the body prior to the euthanasia. Some owners wish to bury the remains themselves (be aware of local regulations, however, which are becoming more stringent) or to have the dog cremated. Others

Renart's Maggie MacPhee and *Ch. Renart's Mickey MacPhee* photographed by Pat Holmes.

want the veterinarian to handle the arrangements. Planning ahead saves more difficult decisions during the trauma of losing your friend.

VETERINARY SPECIALISTS

With a surplus of small animal veterinarians expected in the latter part of the 20th century, and a surging volume of knowledge and medical

Ch. Shajas Rufus O'Brae owned by the author.

technology, many veterinary school graduates elect to specialize with additional courses and training. These include surgery, dentistry, oncology, radiology, neurology, cardiology, dermatology, ophthalmology, theriogenology (reproduction) and internal medicine.

This "overpopulation," naturally, is a boon to pet lovers. If your dog has one of these problems, your veterinarian may refer you to a board-certified specialist or contact one for advice on specialized treatment. Any concerned, caring veterinarian will be happy to do so and assist his patient to live a healthier, fuller life.

Anyone who owns dogs for very long begins to build a canine medical chest. Basic supplies should include cotton, gauze, tweezer, ipecac, muzzle, styptic powder, cotton swabs, rectal thermometer, petroleum jelly, hydrogen peroxide, ear medication, anti-diarrhea preparation, ibuprofin pain killer and one-inch adhesive tape. Include first aid instructions and a poison help sheet with a hotline number.

ETHICS

In all diseases, symptoms may vary from mild to severe. In the most extreme cases, victims may have to be euthanized. Many do live, however, under veterinary care and supervision, occasional medication and owner TLC. Nevertheless, it's important to know which diseases are known to be inherited. Our dogs can carry the factors which transmit hereditary conditions and pass on their afflictions to a higher than normal percentage of their progeny. Affected dogs should be spayed or neutered and never allowed to transmit their discomfort to future generations. Owners should also be aware that AKC regulations specify that surgically corrected dogs may not compete in the breed ring.

Right: *Your Cairn Terrier depends on you for a happy, healthy life. This is* **Abby** *owned by Pat Holmes. Below:* **Ch. Shin Pond Target** *and* **Ch. Shin Pond Rhodes** *owned by Laura DeVincent.*

Books about the Cairn Terrier

The author acknowledges her fellow Cairn Terrier authors whose works, listed below, were a great source of reference and inspiration.

The Cairn Terrier, J.W.H. Beynon and Alex Fisher, M.B.E., revised by Peggy Wilson and Doreen Proudlock, Popular Dogs publishing Company, Ltd., London, England, seventh edition, 1974.

All About the Cairn Terrier, John F. Gordon, Pelham Books, Ltd., and Penguin Group, London, England, 1988.

Cairn and Sealyham Terriers, Mrs. Byron Rogers, Robert M. McBride & Company, New York, 1922.

The New Complete Cairn Terrier, John T. Marvin, Howell Book House, Inc., New York, second edition, 1986.

The Cairn Terrier, Edward C. Ash, Cassell & Company, Ltd., London, England, first edition, 1936.

Cairn Terriers, Colonel Hector F. Whitehead, London, England, 1959.

The Cairn Terrier Handbook, T.W.L. Caspersz, M.A., Nicholson & Watson, London, England, first edition, 1957.

The Popular Cairn Terrier, J.W.H. Beynon, Popular Dogs Publishing Company, Ltd., London, England, first and1950 edition.

Our Friend the Cairn, edited by Rowland Johns, Methuen & Co., Ltd., London, England, second edition, 1933.

The Cairn Terrier, John Woodward, C. Arthur Pearson Ltd., London, England, no date, probably 1930s.

The Cairn Terrier, Florence M. Ross, Our Dog Publishing Co., Ltd., London, England, first edition, 1926, second edition, 1935, third edition, 1937, fourth edition, no date.

Cairn Terrier Breeding & Family Lines, compiled by Alex Fisher, M.B.E., The Marden Press, no date.

Cairn Terrier Records, T.W.L. and Dorothy Caspersz, 1932.

Pedigrees of American Bred Cairn Terrier Champions 1920-1933, compiled by Elizabeth Anderson, 1934.

Pedigrees of American-owned Cairn Terrier Champions 1934-1942, compiled by Frances R. Porter and Clara M. LeVene.

Terrier Type, Special Cairn Issue, compiled, edited, and published by Dan Kiedrowski, La Honda, California, Vol. 25, No.7, July 1986.

The Cairn Terrier Club Yearbook, various editions, English.

The Midland Cairn Terrier Club Yearbook, various editions, English.

The Southern Cairn Terrier Club Yearbook, various editions, English.

The Cairn Terrier Club of America Yearbook, editions 1938-1990.

INDEX

Index

Page numbers in **boldface** refer to illustrations.
All titles have been omitted from dogs' names for the reader's convenience.

INDEX

H-1091, 912 pp
over 1100 color photos

TS-175, 896 pp
over 1300 color photos

TS-204, 160 pp
over 50 line drawings

TS-205, 156 pp
over 130 color photos

H-1106, 544pp
over 400 color photos

TS-212, 256 pp
over 140 color photos

TS-220, 64 pp
over 50 color illus.

PS-872, 240 pp
178 color illus.

H-1095, 272 pp
over 160 color illus.

KW-227, 96 pp
100 color photos

H-1016, 224 pp
135 photos

TW-113, 256 pp
200 color photos

H-962, 255 pp
nearly 100 photos

PS-607, 254 pp
136 B & W photos

TS-101, 192 pp
over 100 photos

TW-102, 256 pp
over 200 color photos

SK-044, 64 pp
over 50 color
photos

TS-130, 160 pp
50 color illus.

H-1061, 608 pp
100 B & W photos

H-969, 224 pp
62 color photos